W9-AQE-645

Curriculum
or
Craftsmanship

129887

Harry L. Gracey

CARNEGIE LIBRARY
LIVINGSTONE COLLEGE
SALISBURY, NC 28144

Curriculum
or
Craftsmanship

Elementary
School Teachers
in a
Bureaucratic
System

The University
of Chicago Press
Chicago and London

CARNEGIE LIBRARY
LIVINGSTONE COLLEGE
SALISBURY, NC 28144

The University of Chicago Press, Chicago 60637
The University of Chicago Press, Ltd., London

© 1972 by The University of Chicago

All rights reserved. Published 1972
Printed in the United States of America
International Standard Book Number: 0–226–30595–3
Library of Congress Catalog Card Number: 71–188235

To My Parents

Contents

Acknowledgments

The study reported in this book was done while I was a graduate student at the New School for Social Research and a faculty member of the Department of Sociology at Brooklyn College of the City University of New York. I want to thank my teachers and fellow students at the New School and my colleagues at Brooklyn College for advice, encouragement, and sympathetic understanding during the preparation of this work. In particular I am grateful to Arthur Vidich of the New School for his wise guidance and patient encouragement throughout the work and to Peter Berger and Dennis Wrong for their help and advice during the latter part of the study.

The field research was supported by National Institute of Mental Health grant MH 9135 to the Bank Street College of Education in New York City. I wish to thank the college for the opportunity to participate in this study and to express my gratitude to Donald Horton, Barbara Biber, and the other research workers there for their cooperation and encouragement during the fieldwork. I am also grateful to Mrs. Ruth Kolbe for her invaluable typing and clerical assistance on the field notes and the immense final report of the Wright School study which was submitted to the Bank Street College Research Division.

Among the most important contributors to this study are, of course, the people associated with the "Brookview" schools, and especially with the "Wilbur Wright Elementary School," in which most of the research was conducted. To protect their privacy, pseudonyms have been given to all people and places mentioned in this book. The Brookview board of education, the school district administration, and the faculty and staff of Wilbur Wright School volunteered to cooperate with this study in the sincere hope that its findings would be useful to dedicated educators in their constant search for ways to improve public education. I wish to express my gratitude to these people and to the children and parents of Wilbur Wright School for their wholehearted cooperation with the study. I hope that its results will give them a useful perspective on their work.

Introduction

In this book I examine the relationship between the social structure of an elementary school and the kinds of teaching that take place within it. The school and school system are formal bureaucratic organizations with hierarchies of power and authority, standardized programs, and routine procedures for elementary education. My purpose is to discover the ways in which this social structure supports and hinders the implementation of different educational philosophies and orientations toward teaching. In the school I studied there were two different educational philosophies, one of which I call "industrial" and the other "individual," and two kinds of classroom teaching corresponding to these ideologies. Most of the teachers—the "production teachers"—are engaged in a traditional curriculum-centered kind of teaching, whereas the principal and a few of the younger teachers—the "craftsman teachers"—are trying to establish a more modern, child-centered educational approach. During the two years of my study I examined the effects of the social structure of the school on the implementation of these two types of classroom teaching and the fate of their corresponding ideologies in the elementary school.

There is a more general purpose underlying this study, and that is to examine the influence of bureaucracy, as a form of social organization, on the work-oriented social actions which are carried on within it. I am interested, in other words, in the general sociological question of the relationship of social form to the content of social interaction. Bureaucracy is the dominant form of social organization in our time, and it undoubtedly has an important influence on the kinds of work we can do and the kinds of things we can accomplish in our groups. This book is a case study of the relationship of organizational structure to the achievement of human goals.

In an attempt of this kind to assess the effect of school structure on classroom teaching it is essential to control for other factors which might affect educational practice. The first chapter therefore sets the stage by describing the educationally relevant aspects of the Brookview community and the philosophies and practices of the educational leaders, including the administrators of the school system and the principal of the school in which the study took place.

The Brookview schools usually receive more than adequate community support, and the leaders of the school system actively promote experimentation and innovation in the schools. This prosperous suburban community values its schools and supports them, and its predominantly middle-class families send their children to school prepared to learn things the school's way. The parents' aspirations for their children's future and the role they see the schools as playing are discussed in chapter 5, which reports the results of my survey of a probability sample of parents sending their children to Wright School. Most parents seem to be accustomed to traditional modes of classroom work and learning, and only a minority are aware of the new individualized approaches favored by the school administrators and being attempted by the craftsman teachers at Wright School.

Wright School was chosen for this study because it has two kinds of classroom teachers. Those I have called "craftsman teachers" are firmly committed to an individualistic philosophy and practice of education. They believe that education ought to be tailored to individual children and carried out through individual or small group projects which reflect the learning needs and capacities of each child. For them the elementary school years ought to be seen as a whole, with children gaining knowledge and skills as they become ready for them and are stimulated by their desire to learn what they have come to need to know under the teacher's skillful guidance. The craftsman teachers therefore see teaching as a highly skilled profession involving constant creative work with individual children.

I have called the other kind of classroom work found in Wright School "production teaching," and it is more usual in American elementary schools. For teachers with this orientation, teaching essentially involves taking a class of children through the prescribed year's curriculum in the prescribed amount of time. They assume that the teacher's job is to see that the children in her charge complete as much of the grade-level curriculum as possible during the school year. These teachers rely on the prescribed school system technology of textbooks, workbooks, tests, and instruction units. They work with drill and repetition rather than attempting to elicit motivation through interest in projects created for specific children in the craftsman manner. The production teachers in effect define their job as administering the curriculum to the children. These traditionally oriented teachers are like bureaucrats, or even production-line workers involved in processing raw materials or semifinished products in identical ways with identical tools. The production teachers must of course take account of individual differences, but they certainly do not try to fashion children's education around their individuality as the craftsman teachers do.

The craftsman teachers and the production teachers work within the same social structure. Both the Wright School and the Brookview school system have bureaucratic forms of organization. The characteristics of bureaucratic organization support the practice of production teachers but seem to frustrate craftsman teachers in their efforts to establish creative, individualized education. In the body of the book I describe these forms of classroom teaching and show their encounters with the organization. I also attempt to delineate how the craftsman teachers and administrators who support this form of teaching respond to their frustration by the system. I think there are lessons to be learned here about the attempt to do individualized work in any large-scale bureaucratic organization.

Perhaps something should be said about my position in the school during the fieldwork for this study. A number of professionals working for the school system spend from two to four days a week in Wright School, as I did during the course of the fieldwork (though I was not employed by the schools). These specialists include the special teachers, the school nurse, the psychologist, and the social worker. Some of them were working for Ph.D. degrees at local universities. I found myself easily accepted by the staff as another professional working in the school. Gradually I gained access to all staff activities, including, most importantly, classroom teaching, principal conferences, committee meetings, and the informal lunchtime, before-school, and after-school conversation groups. The staff came to accept the idea that the benefits of the sociologist's work would come from publication of the studies rather than through any regular contribution to the school's ongoing activities.

The children rapidly became accustomed to my presence, and treated me as they would any other visitor when I came into a classroom or observed on the playground. In their eyes I was not unlike the psychologist, who observed quietly in the playground. In the early grades I was introduced as some-classes and conversed informally with children and teachers on one who wanted to "learn about children and school," and in the upper-grade classrooms I briefly discussed the work of sociologists.

The parents also accepted the idea of sociological research in the school, as is indicated by the fact that only one household in our sample was unavailable to be interviewed in the parent study. The active parents—those holding offices in the Parent-Teacher Association—agreed to be the subjects of a special study themselves. The school staff, the students, and the parents seemed to accept this new role of sociological researcher in the belief that it would eventually serve educational goals. I hoped that it would also contribute to the sociological knowledge of behavior in organizations.

1

The Community and Educational Setting

The School District

Public education is the most important local issue in suburban Brookview, a residential community of 40,000 which is part of a large East Coast metropolitan area. The town was founded in 1924 as a result of a controversy over schools in the local township. The First World War had brought a great population influx to Freeman Township, and, in the opinion of the people in the section which became Brookview, sufficient schools had not been provided. They organized what a local history describes as "an especially bitter campaign waged for the separation of Brookview from the township." Brookview was incorporated and the first official act of the newly elected town board was to create a school district and appoint an emergency board of education to raise money for school buildings. There were about 5,000 persons in the town at this time, and the population was no more than 10,000 at the outbreak of the Second World War. By 1950 the population had jumped to 25,000 and by 1960 it was close to 40,000. Each of these population increases brought diverse kinds of people to Brookview until in 1960 the community had a middle class, mainly Protestant and Jewish but with some Catholics, and a working class which was mainly Catholic and included many of Italian and Irish background.

The emergency of World War II and the reconversion period which followed had distracted the community from concern with educational facilities, and by 1947 Brookview schools were operating on double sessions and facing the imminent threat of three shifts of pupils a day. The school district administrators and the leaders of the college-educated middle class organized a communitywide campaign to pass a bond issue to finance the building of new schools. The board of education approved the superintendent of schools' proposal to contract a professional survey of school enrollments through 1970 and approved a report recommending a school construction program to accommodate all children in single-session schools. A group of leading middle-class citizens organized the Committee for Good Schools and conducted political campaigns in the community to support bond issues offered by the board to finance new schools.

Approximately every two years from 1947 to 1960 the voters were asked to approve new bond issues to raise money for new school facilities. An organized conservative opposition arose, based mainly in the working-class Catholic population but also having the support of conservative Protestants, which generally opposes increased public school expenditures. By 1961 their organization, the Association for Efficient Education, was running candidates in the board of education elections. Two educational political parties now are active in the community, representing class and ethnic divisions of its population. Yearly election of three school board members has become the major area of political activity in Brookview. Each of the education organizations runs a slate of candidates and their campaigns are often bitter and acrimonious.

The Brookview school district today is a large, complex system enrolling almost 8,000 pupils in a senior high school, two junior highs, and ten elementary school buildings. In 1961 the taxpayers of Brookview spent over four and a half million dollars to support this system, or more than twice as much money as was required to run the municipality of Brookview itself. The elected nine-member board of education, on which any adult member of the community may serve, has formal authority for operating this system under the laws of "Seaboard State" and the administrative rulings of the state commissioner of education. It appoints a superintendent to administer the system. The superintendent's staff in 1961 consisted of an assistant for business affairs who was also secretary to the board of education, a curriculum coordinator who served as educational assistant to the superintendent, an administrative assistant, a supervisor of maintenance, and seven secretaries and clerks.

The senior high and the two junior high schools each have a principal, a vice-principal, three or four secretaries, a psychologist, a guidance staff of three counselors, a full-time nurse, and custodial and cafeteria staffs. There are 90 high-school teachers and 105 junior-high teachers. The enrollment of the junior highs is 2,000, which is 400 over their rated pupil capacity, and the high-school enrollment is 1,650 pupils, almost 100 over its capacity. The ten elementary school buildings are administered by eight principals, employ 155 teachers, and enroll 4,250 students. Each principal has a secretary, and there is a custodian for each school. Twelve special teachers serve all the elementary schools, two each in the fields of art, music, physical education, instrumental music, reading, and speech therapy. Four nurses travel between these schools, and three psychologists advise the teachers and work with children in all ten.

In 1961 there were six liberals on the board of education, who generally supported Superintendent of Schools Robert Nelson and his administration, and three conservatives, who fairly consistently opposed him. The liberals generally supported expansion of school facilities, services, and activities which they felt would "benefit the children" and "keep the schools up to date" educationally. They represented those who expected their children to go on to college and who saw a high-quality school system as the most important means of assuring their future. The conservatives had two goals: keeping the cost of the school system as low as possible by opposing expansion of facilities, services, and activities, and gaining control of the board of education in the next election. Since three seats fell vacant each year, they had to elect their candidates to at least two of them to gain a majority of the board.

Superintendent Nelson and the school principals thought board members from both political factions were too closely involved in the details of school system administration. They felt that the board should set general policy for the system and leave the administration of that policy to the professionals they hired. If they objected to the way the system was being run, they could simply not renew the superintendent's contract and could find a man who would run the system to their satisfaction. The educators felt that over the years the board members had come to think of themselves as competent to deal with educational, business, and general administrative matters of the school system in which they did not have professional training, and so thought that the schools could not be adequately administered without their active participation. The educators saw this attitude as an insult to their professional competence; but, although they objected to the job orientations of both factions on the board, they felt they could swallow their pride and work with the liberals, who generally supported their programs.

The Wilbur Wright Elementary School was first proposed in 1954 to alleviate serious overcrowding and end double sessions in the two elementary schools serving this section of Brookview.

Funds for its construction were provided in a bond issue approved by the voters in 1955; construction began soon after, and the building was ready for use in 1957. The population of Brookview, and especially of the Wilbur Wright neighborhood, was growing so rapidly, however, that the new school opened its doors operating on double sessions. This situation was not relieved until two years later when additions were completed on the two neighboring elementary schools which enabled all three to maintain normal single-session school days.

Wright School is a single-story, modern design concrete block structure with red brick facing, consisting of two long, low classroom wings extending in opposite directions from a central body which contains administrative offices and a two-story high gymnasium. The primary classroom wing contains two kindergartens, three rooms each for the first and second grades, one third grade, and the teacher's lounge. The secondary wing contains two third-grade classrooms, three rooms each for the fourth, fifth, and sixth grades, and the custodian's room. All the classrooms are furnished with the most modern equipment, painted in tasteful combinations of bright colors, and have a wall of windows looking out on the campus, yards, and park which surround the school. The administrative body, which joins the two classroom wings, holds the secretary's general office with its files, mailboxes, and mimeograph equipment, the small principal's office, a large nurse's room, a small kitchen with a little room off it which the psychologist uses for testing, a children's library, and a large combination gym-auditorium. The low, sweeping structure is set well back from Brookview Avenue. Over the years Principal Johnson has encouraged classes to adopt projects of landscaping the grounds in front of the building and planting them with bushes and flower beds. A small town park with woods, play areas, and a stream adjoins the school grounds behind and to the east, and the carefully cultivated backyards of the neighborhood's most expensive new homes abut the school grounds on the west. The scene often impresses visitors as an attractive kind of "suburban pastoral."

Hyram Johnson came to Wright School from a nearby community where he had been teaching principal of a smaller elementary school. He was carefully selected for the job of first principal of Wright School, having been interviewed by the superintendent of schools, a committee of Brookview principals, and another committee of senior classroom teachers. Johnson impressed them as an energetic, intelligent man with many new ideas about education and a zeal to put them into practice. Johnson himself saw the new Wilbur Wright School as an opportunity to introduce many of the innovations he thought were needed in American elementary education. Here, he thought, was a new school, excellently equipped, in a new neighborhood with a new population, many of whom are upper-middle-class people who could be expected to support improved education programs, a new faculty, and a new principal. There could be no better situation for carrying out a program of educational change and development. Thus, in spite of the handicap of opening with double sessions, Johnson was enthusiastic about his job and went to work with great energy. Between 1957 and 1961 he accomplished many important educational and administrative innovations at Wright School and attempted a number of others which either failed or had not yet come to fruition. By 1961 Johnson felt he had a school in which it was possible to realize many of his educational goals—but not by any means all of them. He had assembled a faculty which was noted for its intelligence and professional dedication—Superintendent Nelson referred to them as "my favorite faculty"—and with them he hoped to preserve the innovations which had been made and to institute others he felt were needed. Johnson and the faculty agreed to the inconvenience involved in this extended sociological study of their school when they were convinced that the results would probably be useful to educators concerned with improving American elementary education.

Philosophies of Education

Some administrators and teachers in the Brookview school district hold clearly formulated ideas of the goals of education and the most effective means for achieving them. These educators refer to their general educational ideas as "philosophies of education." In the state Department of Education, the Brookview school district, and the Wilbur Wright Elementary School the dominant philosophies of education at the time of the study were liberal, individualistic, and humanitarian, and were derived principally from democratic political theory, the educational thought of John Dewey, contemporary ego psychology, and modern popular sociology.[1]

Universal free public education in the West has as one of its historical roots the liberal democratic ideals of equality and equal opportunity. All men may not be born equal in innate endowments or family class position, according to these ideals, but free public education gives them an opportunity to compete more equally for different positions in society. The educators' idea of equal educational opportunity was expressed in a speech by the state commissioner of education at the commencement exercises of a college near Brookview. He said:

I myself remember when the county superintendent of schools, in the early days of the depression, decided he must take the lead in providing some place for the unemployed youth to go to school. . . . The Emergency Relief Administration provided support which made it possible to open evening college classes in the high school. . . . I read not long ago the list of people now in middle age, leaders in their communities, leaders in their trade or profession, who got their start toward post-high-school education in that inauspicious college. . . .

There is a moral in that, I think, that should interest all of us. Our country is great because of its people. There are many other regions of the world that have most of the natural resources that we in the United States possess and yet they remain undeveloped, the people remain in poverty, self-government is nonexistent, and civilization has passed them by. Much of the difference between those areas and our own country is that in an ever widening circle through the generations we have provided educational opportunity for all, and we have insisted that the door of opportunity should be kept as wide open as possible.

1. An important reason for the mutual selection of the Brookview school district and the Schools and Mental Health Research Program was the similarity of educational values and intellectual background between the leaders of the two groups.

This speech shows a second aspect of liberalism: the belief that general social and economic progress is characteristic of the history of the Western nations and based on the qualities of Western man. In his comparison between the progress and self-government of the United States and the poverty and subordination of the underdeveloped countries, the commissioner does not consider any historical and contemporary causal relations between these two conditions. Western progress is not attributed in any part, for example, to Western domination and exploitation of the underdeveloped world, but simply to the public school system and the "ever widening circle through which we have provided educational opportunity for all" (in the United States). The educators generally see progress toward the betterment of society as coming from equal opportunity for a free public education for all citizens.

The rhetorical focus on the individual, and the development of his capacities through education, relates the liberalism of the educators to their individualism. It calls for an educational program which is sensitive to individual differences in ability and interest and somehow relates learning to them. The Brookview educators feel that schools should first and foremost help individuals develop their own abilities and interests. Principal Johnson of Wright School spoke for the Brookview administrators and some of the teachers when he said, "The individual and his development should always be our central concern." The state commissioner said that he objected to any kind of categorizing of pupils because "within categories there are only individuals who differ from one another"; therefore, he said,

our real challenge and our real opportunity is to see our schools as a whole and to see the children as individuals. Then our task becomes to do for each individual child whatever needs to be done to bring his life to fullest flower.

This conception of education carries with it the idea of a close personal relation between the teacher and the child. Teaching and learning are considered primary social relationships between growing children and the adults facilitating their development. The teacher is expected to be concerned with all aspects of the child's growth, not just his formal academic

learning. The state commissioner feels it is the *right* of pupils
to expect this kind of relationship from their teachers. He told
a conference of parents:

Whatever is good in our schools is almost without exception the
product of a human process, teacher to pupil, pupil to teacher,
understanding one another, respecting each other, and searching
together for what is best for each individual child. . . . I believe
each child has a right to expect that in school he will find teachers
who have a personal interest in him and who care about what
becomes of him.

The Brookview educators sincerely believe that "we need
teachers who give themselves, not just their subjects." They
feel that a teacher should be a kind of "craftsman," who helps
individual children develop their own form, rather than a
"production worker" turning out standardized products on an
educational assembly line. As craftsmen, teachers are expected
to develop strong personal bonds with the children and not
remain impersonal toward their "material" as production
workers do.

Robert Nelson, the Brookview superintendent of schools,
stresses the "development of creative imagination" as a primary service schools could render to children. He views creative
thought as a primary skill needed for life in modern society,
not as a luxury which can be indulged in if there is time left
over from routine instruction. Since rapid change is a fact of
social life today, Nelson feels that education has the unique
task of equipping children to live in a world which will be
significantly different from the present. He holds that to prepare children for life under conditions of rapid social change
schools have to teach children to think for themselves—to
question all handed-down wisdom and to be prepared to discover the nature of the emerging world for themselves. Creativity, in the form of intelligent questioning and original
thinking, is a basic tool for solving the problems of living in
the modern world. Nelson made creativity the theme of his
speech to the opening assembly of Brookview teachers, held
in the high school auditorium in early September 1961. "Schools
today," he told them, "must teach children to think through

problems on their own and not rely unquestioningly on the solutions supplied ready made by adults, even by teachers. I am proudest of you," he continued, "when I hear that Brookview schools are becoming known for students who think for themselves." He concluded by urging the teachers to experiment with ways of developing creative thinking in their classrooms. Nelson was quite serious about wanting a faculty dedicated to helping children acquire the critical problem-solving skills. He chose as his educational assistant a man who would develop a program for helping teachers bring out creativity in the children.

Principal Johnson of the Wright Elementary School shares with Nelson the commitment to providing children with intellectual skills for dealing with a changing society. As a result of his own educational training, Johnson feels that the scientific method of inquiry is the most important skill for understanding the modern world and solving its problems, and that it should be taught to the children as their basic tool for thinking for themselves. Johnson explained this part of his educational philosophy to a new fourth-grade teacher in the following way:

I'm against filling children full of facts that don't mean anything to them and which they'll forget over the summer anyway. I think the schools should teach kids to ask the right questions and then show them how to find the answers for themselves. I would hope that every teacher teaches a way of approaching things scientifically, that is, what we call the scientific method as it applies to everything they do. At the end of the sixth grade, they should understand this method, not be filled full of a lot of unrelated facts. I think in the fourth grade one of the best ways to teach this is to help the children discover the difference between superstition and fact.

Principal Johnson encourages the use of individualized instruction in the Wright School classrooms. He is a modern educator, strongly opposed to what he calls the traditional "lockstep" method of instruction in which all the children in a classroom are expected to be learning the same material in the same way and at the same time. Johnson urges his faculty to shake loose from this and work with children individually and in small groups at a pace compatible with their abilities.

He urges teachers to ignore the formal grade-level curriculum requirements and "take each child as far as he can go" in each subject during the year. This has become the "official philosophy" at Wright School, and when asked her "goals" for the year a teacher will usually begin her reply, "We're expected to take each child as far as he can go in each subject while we have him with us."

Principal Johnson asks his teachers to make learning a creative act rather than a passive attitude. He strongly opposes methods of instruction in which children simply give back, verbally or in writing, something the teacher has just given them, and he tries to help the faculty find methods which involve children in discovering or creating something for themselves. He wants teachers to "foster creative self-expression" in the classroom and "eschew mere rote learning." Education should be a process of discovery and self-discovery.

Saul Levine, Superintendent Nelson's assistant for educational development, is the most thoroughgoing and sophisticated individualist of all the Brookview educators. He believes that schools can help develop unique, integrated personalities in children through a progressive clarification and unification of their values. Levine's ideas come from the analysis of modern life provided by some contemporary sociologists and ego-psychologists. He thinks that the fragmentation of life in which people pursue unrelated activities in unrelated groups deprives modern man of the opportunity to develop a unified self. Having no core self from which to derive standards of conduct, this fragmented man is other-directed, taking his standards of behavior and belief from each of the groups in which he participates. Levine believes that the schools must provide a place where people can develop their own identities. He explained these ideas in a series of discussions with parents and teachers at the Wilbur Wright Elementary School during the fall of 1961. I summarized these ideas and reported, in part, as follows:

My basic idea is that the school is responsible for producing the kinds of people we have. For me the crucial question is, What should be the end product of the school system? Today there are people in every community who are overconforming; they are the yes-men, the people who get all their opinions from the group they happen to be with at the moment. Then there are people who are always acting a role, and it's a different one each time you see them. They don't seem to have a stable identity. Then there is a larger group that is apathetic and listless, like lumps of clay, with no curiosity, no spontaneity, no searching or seeking. And there are many people who are inconsistent, whose opinions on different things contradict each other. How do we explain this behavior, I want to know; for we would like to see our children leave our schools unlike any of these.

These people I have described seem to have nothing inside—I mean no character, no principles. An analyst might say the ego is missing. In education we say values are missing. The person has never developed values which give him a self of his own. Why is this?

In the rural society of the last century, children found the same set of values in all the places they went: in the home, in school, in church, and so on. They also found that adults lived by the values they professed. So the children saw the values carried out in the actions of the adults. In our society, children get different values in the different situations they meet, and they hear one value preached and see people acting the opposite of it. So the child gets a lot of ideas about good and bad, right and wrong, which don't reinforce one another, but are contradictory. This leads to confusion and to other-directed overconformity as a way out of the confusion.

The basic question for education today is, Under what conditions do people become self-propelled, self-directing individuals? I'd say that in the schools we do it by helping the children clarify the values they hold, so they can see how they fit together or contradict one another; so they can ask themselves: Do I *really believe* this? Do I *really want* this? This is the central function of the school—to help children develop values to guide their lives. This way I hope we can help people become self-propelled, self-directing individuals.

The schools, Levine feels, must become the agencies through which society begins to develop inner-directed people with integrated, whole personalities. Teachers, in order to accomplish this task, must become Socratic-like questioners to help children clarify and integrate their values and beliefs.

The Brookview educators strongly believe that the schools should be instruments for improving mankind, and they see education as a mission in the service of humanity. Part of their humanitarianism is revealed in their individualism. However, it extends to mankind as a whole through a radical sociological nominalism in which they reason that since the world is made up of individuals, improving people is the way to improve the world. This belief in the world-bettering mission of education is held implicitly by the Brookview educators. Principal Johnson, however, made it explicit in a brief conversation:

On the way to the superintendent's office for a meeting today Johnson remarked that he thought it was "a wonderful thing" that adult education enrollment was increasing so rapidly in the United States. He was quite surprised when I asked why he thought this was a good thing. "Well," he replied, reaching for words like a man asked to state the obvious, "I just feel the more education people have the better they'll be." Then, somewhat defensively, as if a basic assumption had been challenged, he added, "And I don't know any other way the world is going to become a better place."

The other educators share his assumption that they are working for the betterment of mankind. They tend to regard public criticism of their ideas or opposition to their practices as the result of misinformation or ignorance and to see "education" through propaganda and public relations as the best way to meet such criticism.

The public schools of Brookview were still very much caught up in the Cold War in 1961. The launching of the first Russian Sputnik had led to demands for more instruction in mathematics and physical science and for special accelerated programs in these areas for the brightest students. Superintendent Nelson, however, felt that the survival of mankind depended more on different peoples' learning to understand each other and live peacefully together than on producing more highly skilled technicians to fight the Cold War. As an educator he felt that the schools had to assume the job of promoting this understanding and harmony through study of other groups and contact with people from different nations. Nelson made it a special point to visit the Wilbur Wright School when the faculty was holding a conference on the social studies program. He said he "couldn't stay away when my favorite faculty is discussing my favorite topic," and spent the entire afternoon with the teachers, at one point telling them:

My deepest interests are in social studies. I don't think of it as the geography, economics, or history of any particular area. Social studies for me is the study of man in all his relationships with other people . . . it is basically concerned with the development of attitudes about other people. The purposes of social studies are simple, but nothing is more important to our very survival today. In social studies we want to help children understand other people, especially those who are very different from themselves. We want to help them learn to accept other people. We want to teach them to work together with other people in solving our common human problems. Today it is absolutely essential that people learn to work together to solve their problems. Tomorrow it will be a matter of life and death for the whole world.

Nelson then outlined some elementary school social studies programs which he thought would implement these goals. These included spending a large part of the year doing an intensive study of one foreign society, rather than rapidly and superficially surveying life in many different countries, and perhaps having classes spend part of a year abroad, as individual high-school students sometimes do now.

The educators who hold the liberal humanitarian and individualistic conception of the purpose of education and the craftsman conception of the process of teaching and learning feel that they are in an embattled position today. As the commissioner of education told a conference of teachers and administrators:

Today there is a definite trend toward rigidity, uniformity, and standardization in education, with a lack of concern for the interests of the pupils the schools are supposed to serve. Schools are being pressed to accept the idea that the curriculum should be a sequential series of predigested subject matter packaged by persons who do not know the teacher, the pupils, or their community. Confronted with such a curriculum package, the teacher's role becomes little more than that of a technician . . . pushed up against such a curriculum, many children find nothing there relevant to them and do not learn. . . . So we begin to turn to machines, for some people feel a pupil can be taken through this packaged curriculum by mechanical aids and programming.

The Brookview educators experience constant pressure from government agencies, from people in the local community, and from parts of the educational profession itself to formalize and standardize teaching. Since the orbiting of the Russian Sputnik, they have also experienced great pressure from these same sources to concentrate their efforts on turning out an intellectual elite ready for advanced training in science and mathematics. The individualistic, "child-centered" philosophy of these educators conflicts fundamentally with these pressures toward a mass-production, technologically oriented educational program.

The commissioner described what might be termed the professional nightmare of liberal educators in his address to the éducational conference. He said:

People today seem to have adopted a new way of looking at the young. Children and youth are lumped in with other "natural resources" like timber, water and uranium deposits and the problem [of education] is seen as how we make use of these, "we" being all adults who manage such things. . . . Anyway, the timber goes to the sawmill, the uranium to the Atomic Energy Commission, and the children go to school. There, presumably, children are, like the timber, sorted, graded, and processed, and the theory seems to be that the product will be used in its various forms to keep us strong and protect our position in the world.

The commissioner left no doubt about his opinion of this educational philosophy; he told the conference that he thought "this view of the human being, although currently prevalent, is also thoroughly un-American."[2] This view is the "Brave New World" or the "1984" idea which the progressive educators see threatening their work when they look at the trends of change in the world around them. Here their thinking takes a turn toward sociological realism, for they see social structures

2. During a 1961 school-board election campaign in Brookview, a candidate supported by the conservatives tried to impress his audience with how important he thought education was and how conscientious a board member he would be by saying, "children are part of our natural resources, like atom bombs," and that he regarded being a guardian of children's development as just as important as being a guardian of the development of the nation's atomic weapons.

and forces outside the individual, which he cannot readily influence, setting the conditions of his life. Educators like the men whose ideas have been described here see themselves standing in opposition to the trends toward impersonalization, mechanization, and standardization in modern society, but they do not know how to oppose them, except by trying to persuade the public to allow them to conduct their own work according to their own philosophies of education.

The Bureaucratic Organization of Education

In the Brookview schools, it is expected that education will be conducted in accordance with a set of formal bureaucratic requirements including the regulations of each school, the rules of the school district, and the laws of the state. In some schools, the rules have been collected in handbooks which are revised and enlarged each year. These rules, and the behavior of the teachers in general, must conform to the school district regulations, which are formulated for the elementary, junior high, and senior high schools. The Brookview school administration, for example, publishes a *Handbook for Elementary School Teachers*, which contains regulations and less formal expectations with regard to teachers' work in all the elementary schools. These rules and all other procedures of the school district must, of course, conform to the education laws of Seaboard State and the programs developed by the state department of education to implement these laws.

At the same time, education in Brookview is carried on in the particular context of community educational politics and the administrative policy of the superintendent of schools. In 1961 most people working in the Brookview schools seemed to be aware of the community controversy over control of the school system, and many of the professional people felt that their work and their morale were affected by this conflict. The power struggle was a continuous undercurrent which frequently broke to the surface in vigorous and intensive controversy. In the Wilbur Wright Elementary School, Principal Johnson had strong sympathy for Superintendent Nelson and the educational liberals because he felt they supported his kind of educational program. Teachers who concerned themselves with the community controversy over control of the school board sympathized with the educational liberals, also feeling that this group was most favorably disposed toward the schools. The secretary in Wright School was closely connected with the educational liberals, as was the president of the Wright School Parent-Teacher Association. The custodians of the schools were part of the working class in Brookview, and they supported the educational conservatives. Their group, the Custodial Employees Association, actively campaigned for the candidates of the conservative Association for Efficient Education in the 1961 school-board election. Principal Johnson and the faculty felt that as professionals employed in the system they had to remain publicly aloof from the political controversy, and their professional group, the Brookview Education Association, did not take an active part in this campaign. The PTA officers reported working closely with the liberal party, the Citizens' Committee for Good Schools, for the election of their candidates.

The administration of the Brookview school district is being steadily decentralized under the leadership of Superintendent Nelson. By 1961, much of the school system's decision-making had been delegated to school principals and, through them, to teachers in the individual schools. Nelson and his assistant, Saul Levine, are attempting to create a structure in which professionals at all levels of the educational hierarchy participate in making decisions. Principals are to have final authority over matters pertaining to the operation of their schools, and under the concept of the "self-contained classroom," elementary school teachers are to have authority and responsibility for education in their classrooms. Moreover, the principals are brought together weekly to discuss and decide upon general school system policies, and are encouraged to give their teachers a similar voice in individual school policy. Principal Johnson of Wright School is in sympathy with this form of administration, for he feels that it encourages the professional development of the staff. In the weekly faculty meetings at Wright School, the teachers participate in making policy for the school and even debate school system policies which affect them, sending Johnson to the principals' meetings with their requests and recommendations.

Nelson and Levine hope that all the people participating in the decentralized decision-making apparatus will go beyond simple administrative matters and consider substantive educational issues. They want the principals' group to discuss various educational philosophies and program goals and examine methods for their implementation. They encouraged the principals in turn to administer their particular schools through this group meeting and consultation technique, and to lead the teachers in group discussions of educational policy, including goals and methods of education at their level. Saul Levine was building committees of teachers from each grade level in the system to examine all areas of the school system curriculum and recommend revisions and additions. During 1961, committees were meeting to examine the school system curriculum in mathematics, English, general science, foreign languages and social studies.

Of course, in creating these committees and working with them, Levine and Nelson are interested in gaining acceptance for their ideas so that their educational philosophies can be institutionalized in the programs of the school system. Both men have studied techniques of "group dynamics" and use them to guide the work of these committees. Principal Johnson also uses the teachers' meetings at Wright School as part of his professional development program for the faculty. The people involved in these groups and committees sometimes complain that they are being "manipulated" by the group leaders—Levine or Nelson or Johnson. What to the leaders is an act of indirect leadership toward educational goals is often experienced by group members as an attempt at concealed influence or manipulation. Hyram Johnson and the other principals are in the interesting position of playing both roles—leader and led—one with the teachers' groups of their own school and the other in the principals' group under the guidance of Nelson and Levine. Thus, Johnson may complain that he feels manipulated by Levine at the principals' meeting the same week some of his teachers complain that he is trying to manipulate them at the Wright School faculty meeting.

Nelson, Levine, and Johnson and the other principals who play educational leadership roles in their schools, however, see themselves as attempting to create a *colleague* type of relationship among fellow professionals in the school system through which they can arrive at intelligent administrative and educational decisions by democratic processes. Group discussion and decision-making are to replace administrative surveillance and authoritative command in some of the work of the system. They hope to build a colleague structure among equals alongside the power hierarchy of the bureaucratic system. Because it is taken seriously by Johnson, the colleague relationship is an important part of the social structure at Wright School.

The subject-matter curriculum guides for the school system specify what areas of knowledge and what skills are to be taught and what minimum levels of achievement are expected of the children in each year of school. In the elementary schools all children are given achievement tests at the beginning of each year, which serve the dual purpose of informing the teacher of the test-measured skill and knowledge levels of her class and helping the principal compare and judge the work of his teachers from the previous year. The curriculum is the educational program for the elementary school grades, and the achievement test is the "quality control" mechanism for determining how much has actually been learned. The district requirements for what subjects are to be taught and the minimum level of proficiency are the most important regulations the bureaucracy sets on the work of the teachers. They specify the minimum *content* of the work, whereas the colleague type of administration and the rules and regulations of the school, district, and state simply give some of the *conditions* under which they carry on their work.

In Brookview the subjects taught in the first six grades are reading, writing, speech, arithmetic, social studies, science, music, art, physical education, and health. Classroom teachers in the elementary schools are responsible for instructing their classes in each of these subjects, though they receive some assistance from one or more of the twelve "helping teachers" who service all ten Brookview elementary schools. Since they are so few, these special teachers conceive of their job as teaching their specialty to the classroom teacher through demonstrations in the classroom, rather than regularly teaching the children. This conception is consistent with the idea of the "self-contained elementary classroom" which the Brookview school system administrators feel is the best social structure for education at this level. They oppose any specialization of teaching in the elementary schools, such as is found in junior high and high school.

There is a *Curriculum Guide* for each of these subjects which tells the elementary teacher what she is expected to teach in her grade. These guides also suggest teaching methods for each subject in each grade. The rationale for them is that through their use, elementary education is made a uniform sequence of learning which is always on a level the child is capable of and which can be presented in a way which enlists the children's interests as motivation for learning. As curriculum coordinator, Saul Levine's formal task in the Brookview school system is to see that all the elementary schools teach the required curriculum at least at the minimum level of standards set by the guides. Actually, as we have seen, Levine regards his role more as leader of educational innovation in the system, and he feels that revision of the *Curriculum Guides* by committees of teachers is an important means of innovation.

The *Curriculum Guides* for reading, writing, and speech, referred to collectively as language arts, or just as English, specify the minimum reading vocabularies children are expected to learn in each grade, require the teaching of printing in the first and second grades and of cursive writing beginning in the third grade, and indicate rather vague standards of "proficiency in speaking" expected of children on each grade level. The guides also suggest instructional material for these subjects in the different grades, but here, as in all elementary school subjects, the Brookview school system does not have standard texts which all teachers are required to use. Under the decentralized and "colleagueship" administration of the system there is genuine freedom for each school to select its own teaching materials, and those listed in the guides are no more than suggestions. In the Wilbur Wright Elementary School, freedom to select texts and other teaching materials is extended to the individual teachers in all subjects except arithmetic. Wright School has adopted one of the recently developed elementary school arithmetic programs, and all teachers must teach arithmetic from its materials.

The school system *Curriculum Guides* for arithmetic, science, and social studies also provide programs of study for each year of the elementary grades. The school system arithmetic curriculum is not used at the Wright School, since the new system just mentioned has been substituted. The junior high school mathematics teachers have reported that the children from Wright School know as much or more arithmetic than children from other elementary schools when they reach the junior high. In science each grade is expected to teach material provided in the guides for the seven science subjects: animals, electricity and magnetism, heat and light, plants, simple machines, sound, and the universe. The social studies curriculum for the elementary schools begins in the first grade with the subjects: living in the family, living in the school, living in our neighborhood, and things to do for fun, and continues in the second grade with the food we eat, workers who protect us, and getting from place to place on the sea and in the air. Fourth-grade social studies includes: history and geography of Seaboard State, introduction to geography, comparative study of geographic and climatic conditions, and hero and adventure stories; the fifth grade continues to "expand the child's world" with studies of the history and geography of the United States and its possessions, Canada, Mexico, and Central America, and South America; and the sixth grade "covers the rest of the world": north central Europe, the Mediterranean area, eastern Europe, the Far East, India, the Near East, and Africa.

The *Curriculum Guides* in music, art, and physical education are more general and flexible than those in the other subjects and also are rather dated. In these subjects the special teachers actually create curriculum programs as they work with classroom teachers during the school year. The curriculum coordinator, Saul Levine, is working with the special teachers to develop programs in their areas. So, although there are some general expectations, such as children's learning to play tonettes in the fourth grade, the programs in these subjects are actually in the process of being created by the special teachers under the guidance of Levine.

The school system publishes a *Handbook for Elementary Teachers,* the latest edition of which specifies the required, expected, and suggested behavior of teachers in most aspects of their work. According to the preface it "provides elementary school teachers with regulations, procedures, and other information helpful in the conduct of their work." It is claimed that the *Handbook* was assembled by a committee of principals and a committee of teachers and that "it brings together in written form the practices which have been developed from years of experience in the Brookview schools." State law provides the framework of most of the important requirements for teacher behavior. Thus, for example, teachers must keep Seaboard State registers of pupil attendance for their classes and these records must be perfectly kept as required by the state. (The number of "pupil days" in a year is the basis of state aid allocations to local school systems.) The state requires that a licensed person be with the children all the time they are in school, which means that teachers must never leave their classes during school hours unless a licensed person is available to watch their rooms. State law provides for the minimum number of days schools must operate during the year and the minimum hours of classes which constitute a school day. Brookview school system regulations specify, within these requirements, the days school is to be open and the hours teachers are expected to work.

The formal regulation of teachers' working hours is an especially touchy subject in Brookview, for it violates teachers' images of themselves as professionals, an image which the present school system administration is trying to foster as a basis of high-quality performance. However, conservative members of the board of education express concern about whether

teachers are "putting in a full day's work," and the conservative educational political party in Brookview could make a
public issue of it. The administrators therefore feel that the
statement of "teachers' hours" in the *Handbook* is necessary,
and its wording reflects their embarrassment over the whole
topic. It reads:

The problem of teachers' hours is an extremely difficult one to
approach, for most teachers give fully of their time and effort to the
profession. In most instances they spend far in excess of any minimum standard of hours working with the children and the schools.
Administratively, however, there must be some statement of policy
in reference to the minimum service required of all of us. The
minimum standard of time for teachers' services is established at
7¼ hours a day, including lunch period. In those schools confronted with double sessions, the problem becomes difficult. It will
be necessary for all of us to arrange to be present in our buildings
a minimum of 36¼ hours per week.

Schools which were on double session had, of course, two
contingents of teachers, one working each session.

Teachers' hours are specified more closely both by the school
system and, in Wright School, by Principal Johnson. They are,
at the same time, enforced more flexibly on these levels. The
state requires a minimum of four hours' instruction to constitute a legal school day. In schools on double session in Brookview each "shift" gets exactly this amount of schooling. The
regular school day, on the other hand, runs from 8:45 to
11:45 in the morning and from 1:00 to 3:00 in the afternoon.
Teachers are required to be in their schools a half hour before
classes begin and to remain in school until 3:30 in the afternoon. There is a time sheet in the Wright school office on
which teachers must sign in and out each day. Principal Johnson requires his teachers to be in their classrooms by 8:30 in
the mornings and 12:50 in the afternoons. Johnson, as touchy
as the other administrators about the problem of hours for
professional people, makes a policy of granting teachers permission to leave before 3:30 if they request it, with the mutual
understanding that they will request it only when absolutely
needed. In this way he tries to avoid the professionally embar-

rassing situation of evaluating teachers' reasons for wanting to leave work early.

The most restrictive time requirement is the suggested daily schedule for teachers found in the *Handbook for Elementary Teachers*. It says that "each teacher should use her own judgment in working out her own time allotment," but goes on to claim that "the distribution of time here worked out has been approved in many excellent schools and may serve as a guide to the teacher." The following timetable is suggested for the elementary grades:

MINUTES PER DAY TO BE SPENT ON EACH SUBJECT

Subject	Grade					
	1	2	3	4	5	6
Opening exercises	15	15	15	15	15	15
Reading	100	95	85	60	55	40
Language	15	20	35	35	40	40
Spelling	15	20	20	20	20	20
Arithmetic	35	40	40	55	55	55
Social studies and science	5	10	20	30	40	55
Handwriting	15	20	20	20	20	20
Music	15	15	15	15	15	15
Physical education	30	30	30	30	30	30

The opening exercises had to include at this time a reading from the Old Testament and the Pledge of Allegiance to the Flag required by state law, and teachers were "permitted" to lead the classes in the Lord's Prayer and "songs of a patriotic nature." The thirty-minute physical education period is also required by state law. In Brookview, grades one to three take two fifteen-minute physical education periods a day, and the upper grades, four through six, take one thirty-minute period. At Wright School there is a timetable specifying which classes are to be using which outdoor play spaces at what times for their recess periods. This schoolwide scheduling of recess periods is felt to be necessary because there is play space for only about a third of the classes. The time schedule shows that the teacher is expected to devote some time to each of the listed subjects each day, and it shows her what amount is considered appropriate. In Wright School, Principal Johnson leaves the actual scheduling of classroom activities up to the individual teachers. Each of them has to keep a "plan book," however, in which she lists the activities for each day with the time she plans to devote to each, and this book has to be turned in to Johnson at the end of the school year. This listing, along with the children's achievement test scores at the beginning of the year and brief conferences with the teachers during the year, gives Johnson what he considers an adequate control of class-room teaching at Wright School. He feels that for the most part the teachers should be treated as professionals who know how to do their job.

The bureaucratic structuring of subject units and time units for the elementary teachers provides a framework which, if rigidly administered, would eventually eliminate all spontaneity and creativity on the part of the teacher, reducing her in effect to simply an administrator of the curriculum. On the other hand, the Brookview administrators hold philosophies of education which stress encouragement of freedom, spontaneity, and creativity in the classroom and the development of the teacher as an independent professional worker. In the Wilbur Wright Elementary School there is an attempt to administer the bureaucratic structure flexibly in order to give teachers some freedom to develop their own programs.

The *Handbook for Wilbur Wright Teachers* is a compilation of policies and programs developed over the years since the school opened. It contains eighty-six topics, ranging from the most routine procedural matters to the most complex educational programs. The foreword claims that the book is "essentially a collection of policies and information which were developed by the staff" and that its purpose is "to give aid to teachers concerning procedures and materials in Wright School specifically." The Wright *Handbook* does not replace the Brookview *Handbook* for all elementary school teachers, but merely supplements it for the Wright staff. Principal Johnson always urges new teachers to familiarize themselves with the material in the *Handbook* in order to learn the Wright School ways of doing things. The foreword claims that "the study of the information contained in this book will help solve many problems concerning your work in the classroom and school."

The procedures covered in the Wright School *Handbook* range over such a broad spectrum that summarizing them without distortion is difficult. Their purpose is to achieve uniformity in routine matters in order to facilitate bureaucratic administration and avoid embarrassment owing to inconsistent policies. These procedures include rules of behavior in common areas of the school, such as the hallways, play areas, and auditorium, and rules for the use and care of common instructional equipment, mainly audiovisual aids such as motion-picture, slide, and film-strip projectors, typewriters, record players, and the mimeograph machine. The standard community and state record-keeping procedures are also specified in detail in the *Handbook*. Many matters relating to students are discussed here, including reporting of absence and accidents, behavior in common areas of the school, keeping children after school, safety observations, and tutoring. Procedures regarding relations with parents are also discussed, including the annual Back-to-School Night, notes sent home with children, and conferences between teachers and parents. This summary indicates the range of behaviors it was felt necessary to standardize for the efficient operation of the school.

The substantive matters covered in the *Handbook* include the curriculum and educational policies such as promotion and retention. The teachers are told, for example, that they are free to choose from among the different methods of teaching penmanship, but that the school as a whole uses the Metropolitan City Spelling Curriculum in grades three through six. The entire school adopted one of the new programs for teaching elementary mathematics a year after it opened and the *Handbook* informs teachers of this. It also gives some reasons for its adoption, and the principal's opinion that it is the best of the new mathematics programs. The teachers are also advised that Wright School uses a "continuous progress" system of promotion in which children are kept with their age group throughout the grades and taught in each grade at whatever their academic level happens to be. The *Handbook* informs the teachers that this policy is in the best interests of the children and corresponds with the official Wright School educational philosophy, which requires the teacher to begin instructing each child at his level of academic achievement and to help him go as far as he is capable of in each area of the curriculum.

In the interests of bureaucratic efficiency and educational effectiveness, then, the *Handbook for Wilbur Wright Teachers* further regulates teachers' work and standardizes education even in a school which tries to encourage creative innovation on the part of the staff.

There is a final bureaucratic requirement for teaching in the Brookview School District which is not spelled out in any of the guides or handbooks and is not spoken about precisely as we will describe it here. This is a general, all-pervasive require-ment for quiet, order, and cleanliness in the classrooms and the rest of the school building. This requirement can be ob-served in operation in Brookview elementary schools. The staff, except for the craftsman teachers, seem to assume that effec-tive teaching and learning require an environment which is clean, orderly, and quiet. Teachers who violate these expecta-tions are subject to sanctions from the principal and the other teachers.

Principal Johnson lets his teachers know he feels that litter and disorder in the classroom endanger the safety of the chil-dren and are evidence of a confusion which is inimical to education. Teams of janitors clean the schools at night, and they report to the head custodian any classrooms that are regularly littered beyond what is normal. This information is given to the principal, who may ask the teacher to make a general classroom cleanup the last activity of the school day. Parents in notices from the school are urged to send their children to school "neat and clean, in special school clothes" because this is "conducive to a good attitude toward learning."

Teachers whose classrooms are especially noisy will even-tually get complaints from their neighbors that the noise is distracting children in other classrooms of the wing. All teachers are urged to teach their children to pass quietly through the hall to assembly programs and indoor physical education classes. Principal Johnson discusses training the children in proper hall behavior with each new teacher. Children are expected to be quiet when they go through the halls alone on errands or trips to the toilets and drinking fountains.

Another important sign of classroom disorder is seen in children "wandering around the room as if they had nothing to do," and such a situation is regarded as prima facie evidence that teaching and learning are not taking place. Very little allowance is actually made for any creative disorder that might accompany imaginative participation in classroom activities. The unwritten but very real expectations for quiet, order, and cleanliness serve the smooth functioning of the bureaucracy but probably hinder the development of creative education.

Orientations toward Teaching

Most of the twenty-three women and two men teaching in Wilbur Wright Elementary School during the 1961–62 school year subscribe verbally to Principal Hyram Johnson's "official school philosophy" of disregarding formal grade-level limitations on instruction and teaching children as much as they can learn during the year in all academic areas. In varying degrees, all of these teachers use individual and small-group instruction in their classrooms. Their attitude toward the official philosophy ranges from very mild verbal conformity to strong personal adherence. One teacher, when asked her goal in her work, replied offhandedly, "Well, as you know, we're supposed to take them from where they are [in each subject] when we get them to as far as they can go during the year," indicating a very superficial commitment. Another teacher stated with determination, "My goal is to take each child as far as he can go in the time I have with him," indicating a strong personal commitment to individualized instruction. Most of these teachers see their job as imparting the prescribed school system curriculum to the children, but at different speeds depending on the children's ability and willingness to absorb the material. They are "production teachers" in the sense that they contrib-

ute to producing standardized education as the end product of
the school system as a whole. Four of the Wright School
teachers have more radical individualistic philosophies of education, which they try to put into practice in their teaching.
They are the "craftsman" teachers, in that they try to discover
what each child needs to learn in each area of his life and to
provide experiences through which he acquires this knowledge
in a personally meaningful way. They feel that they must
establish close personal relationships with the children to be
able to help them develop their own interests and abilities—to
build their "selves" or "identities," as Levine would say. The
craftsman teachers are trying to help create unique educational
products.

The production teachers seek, fundamentally, to instill in
the children the part of the total system curriculum which has
been assigned to their grade, and perhaps grades beyond that,
depending on the extent to which they have internalized the
official school philosophy. In this sense, they run curriculum-
centered classrooms. When these teachers do venture beyond
the prescribed curriculum, it is almost always to bring in something they feel the children ought to know about—for example,
a foreign language, classical music, poetry, or international
relations—and not something the children bring up. They are
willing to tolerate occasional brief digressions from the curriculum to some topic of current interest to the children, but
they definitely regard these discussions as divergent and tolerate
them for brief periods only as a kind of concession to the
children. They are very much concerned that the children in
their classes master the grade-level material assigned them so
they will be prepared for the next grade. They are disturbed
by children who do not achieve these standards and are much
less concerned about those who easily master the assigned
material and could go on to more advanced work. The production teachers tend to measure achievement by the ability to
repeat facts given by the teacher or learned from books. The
most conscientious of them are concerned with getting as much
information into the children as possible, and constantly pres-
suring Principal Johnson for additional textbooks, reference

books, and library books. They have no conception of using the children's own interests to motivate learning or of providing opportunities for genuine creative self-expression.

The production teachers participate more than the craftsman teachers in professional improvement activities in the school system, including evening classes in the subjects they teach and after-school workshops organized by the curriculum coordinator to revise the school system curriculum in various subjects, such as English and mathematics. They are more likely than the craftsman teachers to volunteer for such studies and to be "volunteered" by Principal Johnson when he is asked by Levine to supply someone for a curriculum committee. Johnson sees these activities as ways of improving the quality of his own staff, and though he does not think of his staff in terms of the craftsman-production teacher distinction it is invariably teachers in the production category whom he thinks would profit most from these workshop experiences.

The craftsman teachers share the job of imparting the basic academic skills to the children, including reading, writing, and arithmetic, science, and social studies. But their teaching methods and educational goals are the opposite of the production teachers'. In other words, they have different ideas about how the skills and knowledge should be taught and why. The craftsman teachers attempt to develop an educational program from the children's own interests by discovering what the children want and need to know about their world, helping them discover these things on their own, and using the process of discovery as the means for conveying the basic academic skills. They run child-centered classrooms in the sense that they attempt to make learning a creative act in which the child seeks academic skills as tools for finding out something he needs to know about the world. As one teacher put it, this process involves "getting to know the children, getting them to express themselves freely, and using their freely expressed interests as the basis of their work."

These teachers would like to have an entirely flexible curriculum so they could organize their teaching around topics of current interest to the children so they can use these interests to motivate them to learn the academic skills. One year, for example, a craftsman teacher in the lower grades might want to build her curriculum around a house that is going up next to the school, which the children pass each day and observe with curiosity. The next year, however, the launching of an astronaut may be the most interesting thing for the children and the teacher would build her curriculum around rockets and space travel. The craftsman teachers constantly use events in and around the school as material for lessons. A tree blooming in the schoolyard may provide a second-grade biology lesson, and a dense fog through which the children have walked will be the basis of a first-grade lesson in the principles of precipitation. Children will also develop individual and small-group projects, with the teacher's help, which also helps them learn the academic skills they are capable of mastering. These teachers continually pressure the principal for materials not usually considered "academic" in elementary schools—such as large building blocks, ladders, trucks, and trains in the lower grades and plants and small animals in the upper grades. The craftsman teachers feel that the children have achieved mastery on their level of the skills and knowledge taught them when they can use them in their everyday life and relate them to events occurring around them. They do not regard it as learning when children simply reproduce on examinations what they have been given by the teacher or by their books. They feel that standardized curriculums hamstring true education. They are the teachers at Wright School who are most impressed by the Summerhill School in England, because they see it as a place in which each child can develop as a unique being as his particular needs for knowledge are supplied.

Teaching is a mission for the craftsman teachers, as it is for the Brookview educational administrators, including Principal Johnson. The craftsman teachers hold high hopes for education as a means for improving society by facilitating the development of creative, independent individuals. The end product of an ideal education, one gathers from conversations with these people, would be whole individuals with free, inquiring minds and basic respect for the traditional Western democratic, liberal, humanistic values. Since these teachers hold high expectations for their work and make great demands on themselves, they are more subject to disappointment, frustration, and occasional despair at the prospect of being unable to conduct the kind of education they believe in and be the kind of teachers they think they should be.

The career orientations of the Wright School teachers vary considerably, mainly along the lines of age, sex, family status and teaching orientation. All together, about half the staff plan to remain in teaching, about a quarter plan to leave teaching soon, and a quarter are uncertain of their future plans. The craftsman teachers planned, at the beginning of 1961, to continue in teaching or to go into advisory work in schools. Half the production teachers planned to continue classroom teaching or take up special teaching, and the remainder planned to leave teaching shortly to retire, get married, or have children. By the end of 1962, one craftsman teacher had taken a newly created position as educational adviser to the Wright faculty, one had left teaching temporarily in discouragement at not being able to carry out her program, a third was still teaching in the classroom and planning to continue, and the fourth, a man, had begun studies to become a school psychologist. Among the production teachers, two girls had married and moved to another community or left to have a child, two married women had left owing to pregnancy, and the senior teacher in the school had retired, three years before the mandatory age.

Teacher turnover is a major problem, according to Principal Johnson. He can expect to lose a quarter of his staff in an average year, and sometimes as much as a third. He attributes this to the general teacher shortage which, he says, forces him to hire many young girls just out of college who will probably leave in a year—two at the most—when they get married or become pregnant. Johnson also sees a problem in keeping male teachers in elementary school teaching; he is reconciled that, as he puts it, "Whenever I find a good man I know I'll only have him for a few years before he gets ready to move on." It is understood that "good men" move on to other kinds of work because they need more money to support their families and because of the low prestige for men in elementary school teaching. These explanations do not, however, account for teachers' retiring early, leaving for other kinds of work, or quitting in discouragement. Johnson apparently does not see the bureaucratic structure of the school as a source of frustration and discouragement for teachers, especially those with strong craftsman orientations, which might lead to their taking up other kinds of work or leaving the field of education altogether.

Parents' Expectations for Education

Brookview is a residential suburb of white middle-class and working-class families, about one-third each Protestant, Catholic, and Jewish. For Brookview parents the schools are the road to their children's futures. Both middle-class and working-class parents are concerned about their children's education. The future most Brookview parents plan for their children includes at a minimum respectable occupations with secure incomes. Parents of children at the Wilbur Wright Elementary School all hope to send their children to college or to help them get some other kind of training after high school to prepare them for white-collar business and professional occupations. They look upon the elementary school as the beginning of the road toward this goal and are very much concerned with their children's performance in school and the quality of the education they are receiving there, judged in terms of how well it prepares them for further learning in secondary school and college. Parents' attitudes toward the school and relations with the staff are largely based on their judgment of the extent to which the school and their children are living up to their expectations. Parents' expectations therefore constitute one of the basic "conditions of work" of an elementary school staff.

The ambitions Wright School parents hold for their children and their expectations and evaluations of Wright School were ascertained in a sample study of the families sending children to the Wright School. These parents all had college and high-status occupational ambitions for their children. Middle-class families, in which the fathers are mainly professionals, businessmen, and administrators and in which both parents generally have college educations, are definitely planning to send their children to college and plan to finance this education. All of these families plan to send the boys to college, so they can "get up in the world" of business and the professions. Most plan to send their girls to college too—mainly, it seems, as a matter of maintaining their social status, including helping them find appropriate husbands. Parents in the working-class families, in which the man's occupation ranges from skilled machinist to truck driver, many wives work regularly, and both parents generally have high-school educations, say they "hope" to send their children to college. In some of these families the wife's current earnings are earmarked for financing at least one child's college education. These parents feel that college is most important for the boys, to help them "get somewhere in the world" occupationally, and would be a "good thing" for the girls to give them a secure occupation, such as teaching or nursing, and to help them find husbands too.

The study revealed three interrelated tasks which Wright School parents expect the elementary school to accomplish in helping prepare their children for college work and careers. First, they expect the school to concentrate on teaching "basics," that is, what they feel are the fundamental academic subjects. In the working class, "basics" tends to be defined fairly narrowly as reading, writing, and arithmetic. The middle-class parents define a basic academic program more broadly to include science, social studies, and sometimes even art and music. In both social classes, parents expect a "strong academic program" in which most of the school day is spent in formal instruction in the basic subjects. The parents look for evidence of such a program in work brought home by the children, either classroom work or homework they are to do, and in the knowledge and skills the children are acquiring. Often parents compare what their children seem to be learning with what children attending other elementary schools in Brookview seem to be learning. Most parents expect a formal, traditional kind of elementary school instruction, such as they remembered from their own schooling; so their definitions of valid and

acceptable classroom activities conflict with the classroom programs favored by the educational administrators and by the
craftsman teachers at Wright School. Many parents therefore
feel that their children are not being taught as they should
be at Wright School.

The parents also expect the elementary school to teach their
children to like school and to want to learn. Educated, middle-
class parents say they hope the schools will teach children a
"love of learning," whereas working-class parents are more
likely to say they want the teachers to "make them like school."
In both cases the parents want the school to develop in the
children a desire to learn which will motivate them throughout
their educational careers. Teachers are expected to communi-
cate an enthusiasm for learning and to make the classroom
work interesting. The craftsman teachers feel that the standard
curriculum and the formal program of instruction cannot enlist
the student's own motivation and are searching for programs
which can. The parents, however, do not see any conflict between the expectations of an externally imposed, standardized
instructional program and the development of a desire to learn.
They simply feel that crucial attitudes toward schoolwork will
be developed in the children during the elementary school years
and they want these attitudes to be favorable.

The parents' third general expectation is that the elementary
school will teach the children efficient learning techniques. The
middle-class and upper-working-class parents say the elementary school must teach "good work habits" or "good study
habits." The few lower-working-class parents, from families
in which the men have jobs as laborers and less than a complete high school education, say the schools should "discipline"
the children, teach "respect" for the authority of the school
and adults generally, demand "neatness" from the children,
and in general reinforce home discipline. They do not think
that the demand for discipline conflicts with the desire that
children be made to like school. Study habits and discipline
are seen as necessary to success in school and the elementary
school is seen as the natural place to learn them. The administrators of the Brookview system and Wright School and the

craftsman teachers define learning skills as something quite different from authoritatively imposed discipline or efficient techniques for finding information. They see both a desire to learn and the acquisition of learning skills as coming from learning experiences in which the subject matter is made intrinsically interesting to the children so that learning it becomes an activity of their own, rather than something imposed upon them which they do because it has the force of adult authority behind it. Many of the parents know that their ideas about classroom discipline are not shared by some of the educators in Brookview and some of the teachers at Wright School, and they feel that "discipline is lax" in the school.

It is apparent that there are basic conflicts between some school staff members and the parents over the goals and methods of education at Wright School. The educators would agree that the children should learn academic skills, should like school, and should know how to study, but they disagree with the parents on the kind of educational program in which all these goals can be realized. Some educators would also include personality development through creative self-expression among their basic goals of education, whereas the parents see the school as a more specialized organization which ought to concentrate on these other goals.

Conclusions

Public education in Brookview is an extremely complex enterprise when one considers all its various sides: money and politics, educational ideology and practice, the bureaucratic organization of the school system, the various orientations of teachers toward their work, and the expectations parents hold for the education of their children. What perhaps emerge most clearly here are the built-in contradictions in this total system which are bound to bring conflicts into the administration of the school system, its governance by the elected board, and even the practice of teaching and learning in the classroom. The chapters to follow will bring out these conflicts as they appear in the operation of the Wilbur Wright Elementary School.

2

The Craftsman Teachers

The Craftsman Ideology

Hyram Johnson, the principal of the Wilbur Wright Elementary School, and four teachers there—Becky Yager and Alice Davis in the first grade, Hannah Gilbert in the second grade, and Robert Paul in the sixth grade—all share the liberal humanistic and individualistic philosophy of education described in the previous chapter and the craftsman orientation toward teaching, through which they seek to implement this philosophy in the classroom. These teachers have arrived at their conceptions of the goals and methods of education by different paths, along different career lines, and they think about and express their positions in different terms. They do not constitute a group separate from the other teachers at Wright School, but they share a common set of interests and commitments which often brings them together in conversation and puts them in sympathy with one another. Hyram and Becky have had many long discussions of educational ideas and practices since they came to Wright School when it opened seven years ago. Becky and Hannah are friends as well as like-minded colleagues, and they and their husbands often get together outside of school. Robert usually spends his lunch hours with the group of teachers which includes Becky and Hannah and Alice, and he and Becky lead the discussions in this group more than any other teachers. Johnson, since he is in sympathy with their goals and methods, tries to support them whenever this is necessary and possible. This kind of support is very important for a group of teachers holding a minority position in an organization whose bureaucratic structure seems incompatible with their goals.

Becky Yager is the most sophisticated and knowledgeable in the craftsman ideology of teaching. She earned her Master of Education degree at the progressive John Dewey College of Education in Metropolitan City, and did her early teaching in progressive private schools. When asked about her goals in teaching, Becky replied that she "could write books about that." In an attempt to briefly summarize her approach she said, "Practically, I try to provide experiences which will help children learn about the world around them," expressing the basic craftsman methodology, and, "More grandiosely, there are things like imparting one's democratic, humanitarian cultural heritage to the children," alluding to the basic goals of the craftsman teachers. Becky does not feel that teaching involves taking a group of children through a preset curriculum at a prescribed pace. Rather, she thinks teaching should involve creating a curriculum around the abilities and interests of individual children, so that learning is part of their lives, not something separate from their spontaneous interests. Becky described what she would do in her ideal classroom:

In an ideal situation, I would *really* start with the child. I would ask, What does he need to know, and what does he want to know? What is he prepared to know? What will help further his growth? What stage of what period of growth is he ready for? Is it important that he watch a caterpillar crawl along a branch? Mostly, my job has to do with knowledge, with the acquisition of knowledge. I think this should be my primary responsibility as a teacher: to provide them with knowledge they need. Supposing, for example, a child comes in, in a first grade, who is really very much interested in space and atomic development. Well, this kid's probably ready for it, and so he goes on with it. On the other hand, there are other kids, like one youngster this year, who said, "What's a carrot?" Obviously he needs a lot of learning about vegetables, soil, seeds, and experiences with those things. In an ideal situation, for me, I would gauge the kinds of knowledge the children are ready for, determine this for each child, and work with him on this basis.

The "books" which Becky says she could write describing her educational goals and teaching methods have, to some extent at any rate, already been written by the past and present faculty of the John Dewey College. In these publications they present the conception of education developed at the college, which is a combination of progressive education and modern ego psychology referred to as modern education, and their conceptions of the teaching process and the role of the teacher in this kind of education. A very brief summary of some of their ideas is contained in one recent publication directed toward teachers.

The teacher's task is to present the curriculum in such a way that knowledge not only shall be acquired but that it shall become part of the individual's general power to cope with intellectual problems and personal difficulties; that children not only master the techniques for understanding but that they continue to be eager for learning; that they not only be capable of disciplined learning from others but that they gain strength in being able to learn independently through their own activity and initiative; that they not only become aware of a wider and wider world but that they feel deeply and vitally connected with it.

The foundation of the teacher's role in modern education, another publication states, is "establishing basic mutuality of thinking and feeling between herself and the children while maintaining her position as an adult, individually and as an agent of adult society." The modern teacher, it can be said, is a person who has one foot in the child's world of thought and feeling and the other in the adult world, and her task is helping the child cross over gradually from one to the other.

Four basic components of the role of the modern teacher are listed in a recent publication of the college. First, she learns to perceive and relate to pupils as individuals rather than as members of the classroom group. This individual relationship is conceived of as the necessary precondition to genuine interaction, which in turn is the foundation of modern education. Second, the teacher gives the children emotional support in the conflicts they inevitably experience in the process of growing up, in this way helping them acquire "a positive self-feeling." Third, the teacher learns to understand and empathize with the child's thought processes so she can guide his learning toward "the building of the integrative and adaptive functions of the ego . . . she takes responsibility for leading children toward reference systems of reality and objectivity." Finally, she develops a social control system in the classroom which is based on the functional requirements of the children's learning, one that is "rational rather than arbitrary." She gains acceptance for this system through encouraging children's identification with her and the class program rather than through fear and punishment: "The teacher, alongside the parents, becomes a potential identification figure for ego-ideal realization." Thus, on the basis of a foundation in individual relationships with each child, the college people feel, the modern teacher establishes emotional, cognitive, and authoritative ties which enable her to help the child move part of the way from his world of childhood to her world of adulthood. This is the task of the educational process in the elementary school, and the kind of teacher role in which Becky has been trained and which she has tried to carry out in her work.

Hannah Gilbert is the second most knowledgeable and experienced of the craftsman teachers. She graduated from a regular liberal arts college and acquired her craftsman orientation toward teaching while working in a special experimental school in another system. In this school, Hannah said, "I discovered how creative the job could be and really decided education was something I wanted to be part of." Here, she went on,

I got a glimpse of the way education should be. The emphasis was on the child and the individual child. There was individualized reading throughout the grades; and really individualized reading where you have maybe two or three copies of the same book, and that's all, not where you have fifteen or twenty copies of a reader. For the first time here I saw some of the things that might possibly be done in a situation where the emphasis was on the youngster and the material the youngsters created. Here as a teacher you were encouraged to try out new things, you were not only encouraged, you were given real help and support to these things. They *really* wanted you to experiment. There was a feeling, an alertness that went through the whole system; a real self-examination and experimentation, an attitude of [asking] "What are we doing?" and saying, "Let's look at ourselves, let's look at the children, let's not always be satisfied, because this isn't just a job."

As a result of teaching in this school Hannah acquired her educational goals and her craftsman methods of teaching, as well as a feeling of dedication to her work as something that is "more than just a job." Hannah says she wants "to make school a good experience for children, to help them find themselves and to express themselves. . . . I want to help them find a better, a healthier, a happier life, for which they need some skills, but much more than that." In a good school, Hannah felt, "the emphasis should be on the child, the individual child; that is, what he creates and how he develops as an individual, and on the teacher as a professional and on her development." Hannah was willing to stay in teaching as long as she could find this kind of setting for her work.

Alice Davis is new to teaching, but older than both Becky and Hannah. She came into teaching after the last of her own four children passed early childhood. A recent change in teacher qualification requirements in Seaboard State, caused by the nationwide shortage of schoolteachers, makes it possible for anyone with a bachelor's degree to apply for work in a local school system. If accepted, this person then receives a temporary teaching certificate from the state, which she retains as long as she takes four credits of college work each semester until she has accumulated the minimum of eighteen credits in education required for a permanent state teaching certificate. Alice is one of four women with partly grown families who are working at Wright School under this program.

However, Alice is not getting her real teacher training from her courses, but from Becky, who also teaches first grade and whom Alice has taken as a model for her teaching. Their relationship is very much like that of a master craftsman and an apprentice, except that each has her own "shop." During the years of the study it was possible to see the changes in Alice's classroom and in her teaching as she learned the craftsman forms of classroom organization and methods of instruction from Becky. Alice said she took up teaching "because it suited my personal needs in terms of the fact that I like children and like working with small children," now that her own children were no longer small. The craftsman type of education, with its emphasis on close personal relations between the teacher and individual children, its child-centered curriculum, and its prescription of positive identification rather than arbitrary adult authority as a social control mechanism, seems well suited to Alice's personal needs for being close to small children. Alice described the satisfactions she found in teaching in this way:

I find the contact with the children the most satisfying thing; the relationships that are built up over the year. Oh, it is great to have the kids learn to read; you know, to really achieve and go ahead with leaps and bounds and sort of kindle a feeling of excitement about learning in them. But mostly I think the real satisfactions come in the relationships with the children and seeing their growth as people.

Alice sought the closest possible personal contact with the children, and as a means to this she was learning the craftsman orientation toward education.

Robert Paul, who teaches sixth grade, is the only upper-grade teacher with a craftsman orientation. He has a degree in engineering, and became interested in teaching while serving in the army. In Korea, he said, "they needed somebody to teach some classes in slide rule, and as there was nothing else in particular to do, I volunteered." As a result of this experience, Robert discovered he had a liking and a talent for teaching. Robert was released from the army during the recession of 1958 and found friends of his "supplementing their unemployment pay by substitute teaching." Robert described the development of his interest in public school teaching in this way:

So I started substitute teaching and I got interested. I taught junior high school first. And I remembered all the attitudes I had built up through the years about school and I thought I could do something about not engendering these types of attitudes in other kids who were similar to me, perhaps.

Through his contact with school as an adult, Robert acquired a desire to find ways of making school a meaningful and enjoyable experience for children, which it had not been for him. Recalling his own childhood feelings about school, Robert said,

I wanted to make school a rewarding experience for the kids, especially the kids like I remember I was. I loved school but hated the teachers. I was always wanting to do things, to find things out, to learn things. The teachers were, you know, cranky old biddies, always annoyed, always punishing you, then constantly bringing it up over and over again: "Remember the time . . .," you know. They didn't care if you wanted to know something. They just cared that you stay in your seat.

Robert wanted to provide children with a different kind of experience in school, with teachers who were allied with them in their desire to learn and to "find things out." He felt that most children were like he had been, naturally curious and seeking, and that he could make school meaningful for them by creating a classroom situation conducive to discovery and exploration. He said, "Teaching is an art. It's personal relationships with children. And really you can't 'teach' them anything; they learn in the atmosphere of your classroom." Robert's craftsman teaching consisted of creating an atmosphere in which children would be encouraged and stimulated to discover the world for themselves, and he would be there as someone to help them in their discoveries. He supplements the regular sixth-grade curriculum with many materials and programs, as we will see, in order to stimulate children's curiosity and encourage their exploration of various parts of the physical and social world. He felt that he could be successful in teaching to the extent that he could get to know the children individually, stimulate and nurture their curiosity about the world, and help them to discover what they needed to know.

These four teachers express their teaching goals and methods in somewhat different ways, using different terms and placing different emphases. But there is a common core to their thinking; a set of common assumptions about the teaching process which constitute the core of the craftsman ideology of education. There is first the assumption that schoolwork should come from the children's lives and be, as much as possible, directly connected with their everyday living and interests. Second, these teachers believe schoolwork *could* be made a vital part of the children's lives with the proper exercise of ingenuity by the teacher and sufficient flexibility in the organization and program of the school itself. Third, these teachers are committed to the idea that the teacher should relate individually to the children and teach each of them on the basis of their individual needs for knowledge and readiness to learn. Fourth, they feel that children's need to learn and readiness to learn can both be stimulated by a skillful teacher who has sufficient time and sensitivity to get to know each child, and sufficient freedom and imagination to create a curriculum styled to individual interests and abilities.

Craftsman Teaching in the Lower Grades

The primary-grade craftsman teachers organize their year's teaching around a series of projects which the children carry out as a class and sometimes individually or in small groups. They hope to involve the children's spontaneous interest and curiosity in these projects, which are the vehicles through which they try to convey the grade-level skills and knowledge. Some projects remain the same from year to year, but these teachers will also introduce different projects each year according to the changing interests of the children. All the first grades each year go on field trips to a dairy farm and a zoo, and the craftsman first-grade teachers, Becky Yager and Alice Davis, make these trips focal points of their curriculum. The year the first astronauts were orbited, Becky found many of her children most interested in space and space travel, and consequently made this a major project for the year. The following year a house was being built next to the school, which interested the children because they could observe the progress of its construction each day. Becky made house building a major study subject that year. Hannah Gilbert's second grade "adopted" a tree on the school grounds, and observed, recorded, and studied its seasonal changes during the year. The purpose of all these projects was to provide intrinsically interesting and meaningful experiences for the children through which they could learn what they "need to know" about the world. Of course the teachers had to make sure the children mastered the required grade-level skills and knowledge of the curriculum. Their classroom work, therefore, represents compromises they have worked out between their ideologies of education and the requirements of the school system.

In teaching the basic skills of the primary grades, reading, writing, and arithmetic, the craftsman teachers work as much as they can with individual children and small groups of students. At the same time, they attempt to maintain order in the rest of the class by requiring children not currently "in group" with them to be working on some project, either something of their own or some part of a larger class project. For the most part, the craftsman teachers have to be satisfied with teaching reading in this individualized manner, and settle for teaching writing and arithmetic to the class as a whole. The class size, from twenty-five to thirty children, the curriculum requirements that a certain amount of each subject be mastered during the year, and the limitations of time all combine to make this compromise necessary. Here again the craftsman teachers must find ways to reconcile their ideal educational program with the limitations imposed by the structure of the organization within which they must work.

In teaching writing and arithmetic the craftsman teachers also attempt to use material which is of intrinsic interest to the children, so that even though they must conduct the lessons for the class as a whole, the children will be personally motivated to learn. Writing lessons almost always concern experiences of the class or of individual children. The teacher asks for sentences "about our trip," for example, or "about something that happened to you on your way to school." A number of these are written on the blackboard for the children to copy as their writing lesson, often with the option that they may write a "story" of their own instead, if they wish. Arithmetic must be taught according to the new system which has been adopted by the school as a whole. Nevertheless, these teachers also try to make this subject intrinsically interesting to the children by teaching it as part of class projects, such as the measuring activities involved in studying house construction. Here as elsewhere the craftsman teachers work in as much of their way of teaching as the organizational requirements allow.

The classrooms of the three primary-grade craftsman teachers reflect the different types of compromises they have developed between their educational goals and the structure of the educational organization. As a consequence, they experience different kinds and degrees of satisfaction and frustration with their work, and in the end respond somewhat differently to their common situation. We shall now take a brief look at their classrooms and discuss their problems and responses, along with those experienced by the upper-grade craftsman teacher Robert Paul.

Becky Yager's First Grade: April. Becky Yager opens the outside door of her first-grade classroom at 8:35 and admits the waiting children, greeting each by name. After hanging up their coats the children go to their desks, look around, talk to one another, watch the guinea pigs in their cage, and look at books. More children come in; many gather around Becky to tell her things, and two clean the guinea-pig cage, turning the animals loose on the floor. At 8:40 the first school bell rings and a boy turns off the lights in the room. All the children go to their desks. Becky says, "Clear your desks." The children become quiet and Becky says, "Calendar helper, tell us what day it is." A child goes to the large calendar hanging on the wall at the front of the room, points to the number, and says, "Today is Monday, April 14," and returns to her seat. Becky says, "Kenny, turn on the lights." The same boy who had turned them off without a command rushes from his seat at the back of the room near the windows to the light switch on the opposite wall, flicks the lights on and dashes back to his seat. Becky now leads the children in a discussion of making butter. The class has recently visited a dairy farm and is going to make butter as a result of what they learned. The children contribute statements about the various stages of butter-making. After this Becky goes to a large lettering paper hung on the blackboard and asks the children for words they will need to write their story about the trip to the farm. As children offer words, Becky asks them to use them in sentences. Most of the children are raising their hands to offer words and sentences. Becky writes six of these sentences on the paper, underlining the special words in each of them. She says to the class, "For our writing lesson today, you can write this story or be grown-up. . . ." The children finish her sentence for her, saying, "and write your own story."

Here the first two activities of the day, the discussion of butter-making and the writing lesson, are introduced in direct relation to the recent trip to the dairy farm. These lessons are an attempt to make classroom activities a continuation of this trip so they will have inherent meaning. An important part of the classroom social control system has been seen in operation, the turning off of the lights. This is a signal for children to go to their desks and become quiet. Kenny, one of the most active and potentially disruptive children in the class, is in charge of the lights, and by this time of the year he knows his job well enough to carry it out at least partly without commands from Becky. He gets a feeling of importance, and a great deal of physical exercise, during the day as he races back and forth across the rear of the room between his desk and the light switch. Becky now has to interrupt this work to carry out required school procedures, the "opening exercises" and an arithmetic lesson from the required text.

A little after 9:00 o'clock, Becky calls two children to the front of the room and they recite the Twenty-third Psalm and lead the Lord's Prayer and the Pledge of Allegiance. Becky plays the piano and the class singe "America." When this is finished Becky comes to the front of the room and says, "Paper helpers, please get out paper and buttons. Children, please take out your arithmetic books." Two girls go to the cabinet and the rest of the class begins talking as materials are distributed. The room becomes quite noisy. Becky says, "Kenny, put the lights out." The children become quieter when the lights go off. After the paper and buttons have been distributed, Becky has Kenny turn the lights back on and says to the class, "Let's have some stories about nine." Children raise their hands, and when called on offer various combinations of numbers which add up to nine. Some of the class arrange the buttons on their desks into these "groups" as they are suggested. Becky holds up cards with various combinations of nine on them, asks children to read them, and has the class make groups of buttons corresponding to them on their desks. Most children are now busy making groups of buttons and Becky looks around the room, asking a few children what groups they have on their desks. After this Becky says, "Open your books to the pages on nines." Various groups which make nine are illustrated on these pages with different objects, such as sailboats and dolls. In response to Becky's instruction, the children circle various groups in their books, such as six boats and three boats. Becky asks some children what groups they have circled. She apparently knows which children will be having trouble with this work.

The required routines and lessons of the school which cannot be made part of a meaningful class project have here been introduced as actual interruptions of the class program, and when Becky finishes with the arithmetic lesson she returns to the class projects and the classroom work associated with them.

At about 9:20 Becky says, "Put your books away. Paper helpers collect the buttons. Put your desks in our science circle,

I have something to share with you." The children push their desks toward the edge of the room and put their chairs in a large circle in the center of the room. When they are seated Becky picks up the topic of milk and the making of butter which the class discussed earlier. Then she reads an article from a Metropolitan City newspaper concerning two new lion cubs born at the zoo. She shows a picture of the cubs around the circle. The children begin to get restless, and begin to talk and poke one another. Becky says, "Put your hands in your laps and think of a question you would want to ask if you went to the zoo." A few questions are suggested, but the children become more restless and begin to poke and wrestle with one another again. Becky says, "Quietly put your desk and chairs back." The children jump up, shove, and whoop. Becky says, "Kenny, put out the light." The noise gradually subsides and Becky says, "Let's get ready for our writing lesson." Children take pencils and lined paper from their desks as Becky continues, "Turn on the lights. All fold your hands on your desk for a minute." She then reviews the instructions for the writing lesson—"either write your own story or copy the one we wrote"—and most of the children begin writing with intense concentration. As they work Becky goes around the room helping them spell words they want to use and admiring their work. A child who wants to use a word he cannot spell raises his hand. Becky goes to him and asks him to use the word in a sentence. If he is using it correctly, Becky writes the word on the blackboard for the child to copy into his story. Children show each other their stories, and some begin to draw pictures to illustrate their stories.

In this sequence, Becky has brought the children back to the project in which they are currently engaged, evolving out of their trip to the dairy farm, and introduced the topic of their next trip, which will be to the Metropolitan City Zoo. The abstract idea of this new project, however, holds the attention of the children for only a few moments. Becky is not surprised, since this is the first introduction of the idea. More discussions will be held, and more work done in preparation before the actual trip is undertaken. The trip will be followed by a series of related activities such as those being carried on now in conjunction with the past farm trip. Becky returns the class to work stemming from the farm trip—the writing lesson for the day—when their tolerance for the abstract idea of the zoo trip has been passed and they become disruptive. The writing lesson, it should be noted, is totally effective in restoring order to the class, as the children get down to work on something which seems to be interesting to most of them. If they elect to write their own stories, the only limitation on the words they are allowed to use is their *need* for the word to express what they want to say. As we will see later, Hannah Gilbert uses a similar procedure in her second grade, except that instead of writing the word on the blackboard she prints it in the child's own "dictionary," a small notebook he keeps for all the new words he uses in his stories. Children are acquiring a vocabulary of words which are meaningful because they *need* them to express a part of their experience. Language skills are being taught in these classes as intrinsic parts of children's experience, not as abstract technical exercises.

It is 9:50 when Becky calls the first reading group to the "reading circle," a group of chairs under the windows, separated from the classroom by a long, low bookshelf and walled off from the block-playing area by the piano, which extends lengthwise into the room. About a third of the class gathers in this area, and Becky conducts a reading lesson with them while the remainder of the class writes, draws, or plays with blocks or with the guinea pigs. Fifteen minutes later Becky sends the reading group back with the instructions to "get out your workbooks," and a new group immediately assembles in the circle. As she instructs them, Becky occasionally asks a noisy child in the room to "be more quiet, because it's awfully hard for us to hear our words." All four guinea pigs are out on desks, children are building with the blocks on the other side of the piano, others are cutting illustrations from magazines, and some are coloring or playing with clay at their desks. Becky has the reading group do some writing; they sit on the floor and write with the paper on their chairs. When they are busy she leaves them and asks two children to "take the mural out into the hall." A boy and girl get a long sheet of brown paper and jars of paint and brushes from the shelves at the back of the room and carry them into the hall. The painting is a partially completed class mural depicting the dairy farm they recently visited. Becky goes into the hall with the children, closing the classroom door behind her. The children in the room continue with their activities. When Becky returns she asks the reading group to return to their desks, and another group assembles in the circle. Becky plays a word game with this group, which has only four members. She occasionally reprimands children who are not working at their desks. Most are at their desks, conversing occasionally with their neighbors. Some children wander into the reading area to get books. Three or four others watch the lesson. One comes and sits in the circle. Becky asks him if he wants to visit. She asks one of the group to give him a book and tell him what page they are on, and carries on with the lesson. The remainder of the class is still involved in various activities. Some talk to each other and walk about the room. Becky starts the reading group on their workbooks and says, "Kenny, turn out the lights." When they are off she asks individual children what they are working on, and if they give an acceptable activity in reply, Becky asks them if they will please do it at their own desks. Then she has the lights turned back on and goes to the cabinet over the sink to get out cookies for milk-and-cookie time.

Becky has succeeded in spending most of the morning working with children in small groups, and after milk-and-cookie time she will spend fifteen minutes with yet another reading group before it is time to get the children ready to go home for lunch. During the snack time Becky reads the class a story about some animals at the Metropolitan City Zoo, as another step in preparation for their forthcoming trip. Each possible moment of the day is put to use in the service of the project-organized instructional program and the goal of individualized instruction in a classroom of twenty-five six-year-old children.

Becky is not, however, satisfied with her work. She is unable to achieve her teaching goals, she says, "with these particular children in this particular time and place." Becky feels very strongly the discrepancy between her goal of individualized instruction using material which is meaningful to the children and the organizational necessities of group instruction and the required curriculum. In the public schools, Becky says, "I cannot come close to my ideal situation of teaching each child according to what he needs to know and is ready to know." There is too great an emphasis on the acquisition of "empty skills" in the first grade, Becky feels, from the school, the parents, and the children themselves. She described the problem in this way:

First, the curriculum we are given is not centered on child interests and needs. Then the children themselves have certain expectations of school, because of the community in which they live, their parents' attitudes, and reports from their older brothers and sisters, which don't go with the kind of teaching I think is right. Then, the parents have certain expectations of what the curriculum ought to be, which I feel is a rather rigid approach; for example, that in first grade you study one and one are two, you study one hundred words or three books, and this makes up education.

The school system which defines her task—the teaching of the curriculum—and the people with whom she must carry it out, the children and their parents, all tend to define early childhood education as a formalized set of routine activities, whereas Becky tries to make it an intrinsically meaningful part of the children's lives.

A second and equally serious source of frustration for the craftsman teachers is the social structure of the organization within which they are trying to realize their goals. They, along with the other teachers, are required to conform to the school's requirements for cleanliness, order, and quiet in the classroom, and they must maintain sufficient order among the majority of the children to enable them to spend some of the day working with the small reading groups. Becky, it will be remembered, required each child not "in group" with her to be at work on some project which kept him at his desk. She had instituted a highly structured system of social control in the class which enabled her to spend much of the day working with the children in groups, but which at the same time severely limited the freedom of expression and activity of most of the children in the class for much of the day. Once this structure is established, Becky controls individual children by calling them to account for their activities in terms of the classroom rules and routines. When necessary, she has the lights turned out and reminds the class as a whole of the rules under which they are supposed to be operating.

The craftsman teachers feel most keenly the contradiction between the desire to relate personally to individual children, which is the first goal of their teaching orientation, and the necessity of organizing their classes into smoothly functioning groups to maintain order. This order, as all teachers discover in their first year, is essential as a prerequisite to teaching and learning in the classroom. Its creation, however, precludes personal relationships with individual children, because the class must first be related to as a group, and then the children are related to as members of this group—that is, in their role as pupils rather than in their individuality. In sociological terms, Becky has learned what every teacher must learn, regardless of her philosophy or orientation; that twenty to thirty children in a classroom must first be organized into a functioning group before they can be taught the curriculum, and that this ultimately means that the teacher relates to the class as a group and to its members in their roles as pupils. The organizational structure of the school negates the key craftsman goal of individualized instruction.

The primary-grade craftsman teachers have responded differently to this fundamental conflict between their teaching goals and the organizational requirements. Hannah Gilbert has created a more formal and structured classroom organization than Becky has, whereas Alice Davis is trying to work within a much less formal, and consequently much more chaotic, classroom organization. Let us look briefly now at these two classrooms.

Hannah Gilbert's Second Grade: December. It is a dark winter morning. Hannah is conducting reading lessons with individual children at a table by the windows. As a child reads to her she keeps the others in the class, who are reading at their desks, in order by calling out the names of those who talk to their neighbors. Each child reads to Hannah for a few minutes, then she asks him questions and sends him back to his desk to continue work. One boy is continually talking, and Hannah finally makes him sit by her. After a number of children have read to her Hannah gets up and goes to the front of the room and says, "All right, put your work away. We have something to talk about." The children stuff their books and papers into their desks and look up in anticipation. Hannah says, "Remember, we are going to have a party next week . . . ," at which the children clap, bounce in their chairs, and call out, "Goody!" Hannah continues, ". . . and we have to decide what kinds of refreshments we want to have." The children begin suggesting foods and are soon vying with one another to see who can think up the most elaborate kinds of refreshments. Hannah says, "All right, time for class news now." A few children shift their attention to the new topic, and others continue with what has become the food suggesting game. There is a great deal of noise, but Hannah is unconcerned as she tapes a large piece of writing paper to the blackboard. When it is ready she turns to the class and says, "All right, one, two, three" and the class quiets immediately. "Who has news?" she asks. Half the children in the room raise their hands, straining to be called on. As Hannah calls on them, they each give a sentence, which she writes on the large paper. These include, "On the way to school a dog chased me"; "Next week we are having a party"; and "Smokey is afraid of the dark." (Smokey is the class pet rabbit who panics whenever the shades are lowered for showing movies or film strips and therefore has to be taken out of the room during these programs.) When there are six of these sentences on the board, Hannah calls an end to the contributions and goes over them underlining new words and letter combinations and questioning the children about them. The paper monitor is giving out lined paper to the children, and they begin to copy the sentences as their writing lesson.

The compromise nature of Hannah's classroom is quite evident here, as she keeps most of the children under very rigid control at their desks while she has children read to her, not in groups, but singly. An activity which threatens to become disruptive is simply replaced by another which is used to call the children rigidly to order. Within the structure of this strict order which she enforces, Hannah builds a writing lesson from material submitted by the children from their daily experiences. Hannah has created a highly structured organization in her room through which she controls the class and keeps the children busy so she can spend most of the day working with individuals. Hannah described the compromise she has worked out between her teaching orientation and the requirements of the school in this way:

When I first came here I wanted to continue to do this individualized reading and I asked Hy [Johnson, the principal] about this; not whether I could, but what were some of his feelings. I guess I wanted to know mainly because I didn't know the reactions I might get and I wasn't prepared to tackle the parents alone [if they should complain]. He said I could have the program if I could guarantee that the children would get the skills in the basic reader. I felt I couldn't guarantee this in this system so I worked with a modified program of grouping and smaller groupings.

Later, Hannah said, Johnson told her she could use any system she "felt comfortable with" but by this time she had developed her compromise program. She had introduced as much individualized instruction as she felt she could, and was devising projects, such as the class adopting a tree and recording its seasonal changes or taking a pet rabbit and studying its care and development, which she felt would elicit children's spontaneous interest.

Hannah has learned through experience to work out her programs of instruction without calling them to the attention of those in authority, so she can maintain some autonomy within the structure of the school and the system. Demonstrating unusual organizational sensitivity, Hannah explains her procedure in this way:

Sometimes I think the less we ask, the better off we are. If we ask if we can do things we want, if you always ask permission, the principal will have to give the "right answer" because he is now responsible for whatever you do, for its success or failure. I think if you take the initiative and do things by yourself, provided you have a good sound basis for doing it and you can work well with the group you have a chance of getting some things you want. Then, if you succeed, it's fine, you're praised and you are said to have initiative and to be a good teacher. If it fails, so you're called on the carpet once or twice. But if you always ask, you may never get a chance to see if it would succeed.

By sparing the principal responsibility for her innovations, Hannah feels she can introduce more of her own ideas into her teaching, provided she is sure of what she is doing educationally and has a "good" relationship with the class.

A basic part of the relationship needed for her kind of teaching, Hannah points out, is an organization through which she can control behavior. Hannah reports spending the first six or seven weeks of the school year just organizing her class so they can spend the remainder of the year learning. First, Hannah says, "I spend the beginning of the year on work habits rather than on work, in establishing our work routines." She begins with very simple lessons for the class as a whole with the sole purpose of training the children "in the way we work, the way we move from one activity to another, in the ways we solve some of the problems that come up" during a class day. Hannah then systematically establishes a morning work routine "so that I have a block of free time to work with individuals and reading groups." Morning routine begins with one task given the class, in writing or arithmetic, for example, which they are to carry out at their desks while Hannah works with reading groups. Then a second task is added, and a third, and finally by spring the children are doing four assignments on their own each morning while Hannah conducts the individual and small-group lessons.

Hannah feels very strongly that in spite of her efforts, she cannot carry on the kind of education she believes in. Referring to her work as a whole she says, "I can't have my own program, but at least I'm doing what I can with theirs." As a teacher with a strong craftsman orientation, she feels truly alienated from the rigid classroom organization and standardized teaching she must use in this educational bureaucracy.

Alice Davis is the least experienced of the craftsman teachers and is still learning the craftsman orientation and its techniques from Becky Yager, whom she talks with during the day, and from Principal Johnson, with whom she has long conferences after school. It is possible to see the gradual change of Alice's work during the year as she acquires the humanistic, individualistic philosophy of education and begins to learn and put into practice the craftsman methods of teaching. Alice does not, however, as we will see, learn the necessary compromises between these methods and the requirements of order, quiet, and cleanliness imposed by the organization. As a consequence, her room shows a disorder and confusion not found in Becky's and Hannah's rooms.

Alice Davis's First Grade: November. It is the middle of a morning and two rows of children are sitting in a semicircle in front of Alice at the front of the room carrying on a reading lesson. The rest of the children are engaged in various activities; building with blocks at the back of the room, cutting colored paper at their desks, or playing with toys and games on their desks and the floor. The children are rather noisy and distract those in the back row of the reading group. At least five children approach the visitor and ask him questions. When asked if they aren't supposed to be doing something, they tell him no. After there has been a great deal of noise and moving about in the room, Alice says softly, "I'm sorry, but you're out of order. Take your seats please." One group of children disperses. Alice seems exceedingly tolerant, almost never calling down a child or disciplining the class, and generally tolerating a very high level of noise and movement in the room. The noise level soon begins to rise again, and Alice finally tells the three loudest children to put away the guinea pigs they are playing with and put their heads down on their desks. The children, in response, take the guinea pigs to their desks and play with them there, obeying in a fashion. Alice dismisses the reading group and says, "Please take out your writing now." She goes from child to child checking the work. She seems almost to engulf each of the children as she leans over them at their desks and examines their work.

Alice is seen here working with a very large reading group in a rather formal arrangement of two rows of chairs facing her, while she faces the group and the class from the traditional teacher's position at the front of the classroom. However, she avoids as long as possible imposing her authority on the disruptive children, obviously wishing to avoid it completely. She does refrain until the class can no longer function because of the commotion in the room. The reactions of children to the presence of another adult, such as the janitor, principal, or observer, is a very accurate measure of the strength of a teacher-imposed social order in a classroom. The observer, for example, was completely ignored by the children in Becky's and Hannah's rooms, whereas the children in Alice's room, and one or two others in the school, tried to make him a major focus of attention. When the custodian comes in to empty the wastebaskets (he does this each morning in the lower grades to remove the papers the children have cleaned from their animal cages before they begin to make the rooms smell), he is ignored in the rooms of the more experienced teachers, but almost every child in Alice's room greets him at least once by name. The children in Alice's room have not been organized into a set of activities which will keep them quietly occupied while Alice works with the reading groups. The changes in the class over the year are indicated in the following observation from the last weeks of school.

Alice Davis's First Grade: Late June. At 11:00 Alice is reading with four children in a reading circle which has been arranged under the windows, just as in Becky's room. The rest of the class are working or playing about the room. Two girls have the class guinea pigs on their desks. Two boys are riding large toy trucks loaded with blocks toward the block corner, which is also by the windows, separated from the reading circle by the piano standing lengthwise into the room, as in Becky's classroom. There is a great deal of talking and walking about the room. Only two or three children are sitting at their desks. Two or three are playing on a small jungle gym in the coatroom. Seven or eight gather around the visitor to watch and question him. Some bring things they have made to show him, obviously wanting to be admired. They begin to drift away to other activities only when they find me uncommunicative. Alice is now playing a word game with the four children in the reading group. Two boys clean the guinea-pig cage and begin washing desks. The children playing with blocks begin throwing the hollow cardboard ones, making quite a noise. A boy asks the three playing with the blocks, "Why are you playing with the blocks?" One of them replies, "Mrs. Davis said we could." He goes away and returns in a minute saying Alice has given him permission to join them. Three children have wandered into the reading area and informally joined the reading group, which is continuing its word game. A boy riding by on a truck says to the visitor, "That's an awful long story you're writing. Where're you going to send it? To a magazine?" The observer shakes his head and the child says knowingly, before riding off on his truck, "I know, you're just going to give it to Mr. Johnson" (the principal). Five children, following the lead of a girl, are making hats of folded paper. A group of girls raids the boys in the block corner, demolishing their structure. A number of children have gathered in the coatroom and are arguing loudly. Alice leaves the reading group, crosses the front of the room, and chases the children out of the coatroom. On her way back a number of children complain to her about the behavior of other children. When Alice reaches the reading group more children have joined it, and many in the room are shouting. She says, "Shhh," but this has no effect. She says, "The talking is too loud, we cannot work." The shouting stops. Alice dismisses the reading group. The children from it wander about the room boasting about how many times they won the word game. Alice goes to her desk at the front of the room and rings a little bell, just like the one Becky has on her desk. She says, "Clean-up time now." There is no noticeable change in the children's activities. Alice begins calling them by name. A few sit, but then get right up again. Alice is urging them to clean up the room and go to their seats. A boy rolls on the floor at the back of the room crying and holding his head. Another calls to Alice, "Mary hit him." Alice rushes to the crying boy as Mary says defensively,

"Jerry hit me first." Many children gather around. Mary has hit Jerry on the side of the head with a wooden block, and he is in real pain, as well as being extremely angry. Alice sends him to the nurse's office with two other children and insists that those who aren't cleaning up go to their desks. They sit and get right up again. They begin to gather around the visitor, and he leaves at 11:35.

Alice, it can be seen here, is attempting to employ the craftsman teaching technology without first creating an organization to control the majority of the class while she works with individuals and small groups of children. In fact, Alice found her work frustrating when she was forced to play an authoritative role because this got in the way of the close, loving relationships she sought with the children. She describes her frustrations in this way:

I think the most frustrating thing is probably the largeness of the group and your inability to be what you feel you should be in the situation and do what you feel you should do or would like to do. The unwieldiness of a classroom situation, because we have as many kids as we do, means I am forced into being a different kind of person from a disciplinary point of view, or, you know, the authority figure that I really don't enjoy being. The whole classroom situation has to be a good deal more formal than I would want it because of the largeness of the group.

Alice feels that she should be more of an authority figure than she would like to be, and she recognizes the necessity of organization even though she creates only a very loose one.

Though she regrets even the very loose organization she is forced to impose and the times she does play the authority role, Alice obtains a great deal of personal satisfaction from the relations she creates with the children. Alice stated that the contact and personal relationships with the children were her main sources of satisfaction. She has, by the end of the year, developed close, loving relationships with individual children, from which she gains immense personal gratification. There is no doubt that the loose structure of her class, which permits disorder and accidents, and her reluctance to be an adult authority figure, which contributes to the chaos of her room, help the development of these relationships. Alice is by far the happiest of the craftsman teachers at this point in her career. When other teachers take their classes to the play area in the park behind the school, they walk at the head of a long line of children who are pulling wagons, carrying balls, cars, jump ropes, and other toys, and occasionally hopping, skipping, and talking to each other. By springtime Alice's class surrounds her in a running, jumping, shouting, turbulent mass of children, and she clasps a child tightly to her sides with each hand as they move toward the play area, her face positively radiating her happiness. She has won the love of the children, and this is apparently what she wants from her work.

These three lower-grade craftsman teachers, with their similar philosophies of education and orientation toward teaching, have responded differently to the problems experienced in their work. There is, in fact, a very interesting correlation between the amount of teaching experience they have had, the degree of order and organization in their classrooms, and the degree of satisfaction they receive from their work. Becky Yager and Hannah Gilbert are the most experienced of the three, whereas Alice is only in her first year of teaching. Hannah's classroom is the most orderly and most highly organized, Becky's is the next most organized, and Alice's room shows a great deal of disorder and confusion. Of the three teachers, Alice is happiest in her work, Becky is rather dissatisfied and looking for more "challenging" forms of schoolwork, as she puts it, and Hannah is positively alienated from her work and planning to leave teaching, at least temporarily.

The year after the study, Becky had taken a newly created position of "resource teacher" in the Brookview elementary schools, and was working at Wright School as a general adviser to all the teachers. Becky said she had done all she could to realize her professional goals in the classroom, and that for someone committed to the profession of education this meant she had to find another role, as she put it, "In which I can continue to grow professionally." She was looking forward, she said, to working with other teachers to see how much of her teaching orientation could be incorporated into work on different grade levels. Hannah Gilbert, on the other hand, left school and described herself as "staying home for a while to think things over." Later she began looking around for the kind of school in which she might be able to implement her philosophy of education and teaching orientation. Alice Davis remained in the first grade, continuing to learn the craftsman orientation from Becky, who was now in a formal advisory capacity.

Craftsman Teaching in the Upper Grades

Robert Paul, the only upper-grade teacher with the craftsman orientation, could assume that his sixth graders were competent in the basic academic skills and sought to nourish an intellectual curiosity which would motivate them to use these skills to explore the parts of the world which were important to them. Robert had gone into teaching with the idea of helping curious, seeking, motivated children learn what they wanted to know. He has created the fullest, most interesting, and most varied classroom in Wright School; it seems to overflow with things to see and do, to help arouse and satisfy the pupils' intellectual curiosity. Ideally, he would like the children to see him as someone who is ready to help them find out what they want to know.

Robert Paul's Sixth Grade: January. Maps of Europe and pictures of its cities and countryside cover the bulletin board across the back of the room, illustrating the current social studies project. Plants are lined up along the windows and scattered on tables about the room. Reference books on various European countries are displayed on a table by the windows. There are a number of simple electrical demonstration devices on a table at the back of the room, connected with an assortment of wires, batteries, and switches. A chart on the wall by the door shows the European countries which different children are to report on, and the dates of their reports. Fish tanks gurgle on the counter next to the sink, and white mice hide under the newspapers in their wire mesh cage. The children are working on arithmetic. There is a mathematics puzzle on the blackboard at the front of the room. Four girls are seated around Robert's desk working with him on some seventh-grade algebra. A boy who apparently is an advanced math group of his own works a very involved problem at the blackboard. The rest of the class are at their desks working on problems from their texts or drawing and coloring geometric figures. There is an undertone of conversation and children occasionally leave their desks to get materials from the cabinets or go out of the room, presumably to the drinking fountain or the toilet. Robert dismisses the advanced math group, and as they go to their desks several children come up with questions. He speaks briefly with each of them and then calls two boys to bring their work to him. They are apparently working from a fifth-grade text. Robert checks their work and sends them back to their seats. He then gets up and walks around the room looking at children's work and answering their questions. He talks briefly with the boy who is working at the blackboard. Children who have finished their work are trying to solve the puzzle on the blackboard. They compare work and converse quietly. Robert says, "Who has the answer to the challenge?" A number of children, mostly girls, raise their hands. Robert calls on three and each gives a different solution to the puzzle. Each answer is met with cheers from some students and moans from others, who then demand to be allowed to give their answers. About half the class is watching and participating, while the rest continue to work from their books. As it becomes evident that the different answers have strong partisans, more stop work to watch the argument. Robert writes the answer from his book. Three or four children are so sure of their different answers that they challenge him. One says, "Did you put it up right?" indicating the puzzle on the board, and another adds, "I think you made a boo-boo." Robert checks the problem on the board with the book and says it is written out correctly. He then begins a discussion with the class of how they arrived at their different answers.

Robert can be seen here working with different children at their different levels of arithmetic achievement while at the same time trying, through the day's puzzle, to stimulate interest in mathematics itself as a challenging intellectual world as well as a required school subject. Arithmetic is probably the most difficult subject in the curriculum to make meaningful for the children, and in most cases, Robert reports, he does not succeed. A few, those in the advanced groups, are interested enough in the subject to work at it, but most are just getting by with what they must do, or less. Robert, because of his engineering background, is particularly interested in mathematics and science, and it pains him a great deal to teach arithmetic "just as a set of empty skills"; but, he feels, "this is just what it's going to be for most of the kids and there's nothing you can do about it." In an ideal school situation, he says, children would be taught various kinds of math as they needed it to carry on work in which they were engaged, "as in the Summerhill School in England." The following observation illustrates more problems which Robert finds in trying to implement his craftsman orientation toward teaching.

Robert Paul's Sixth Grade: The Middle of June. The children are at their desks working individually and in small groups using various social studies reference books. The six rolling carts of encyclopedias used in the upper grades are in the room, and a chart by the door lists the countries of Africa and the children who are to report on them and the dates of their reports. Robert is seated at his desk talking with a boy who is protesting the grade he has received on his report on an Asian country. The boy received a B and feels he should have an A. He tells Robert he included everything he was supposed to in the report, to which Robert replies that he was supposed to put the material together "so it told a whole story" and not just "list unrelated things one after another." The boy listens and as soon as Robert finishes begins arguing that these expectations are unfair. Robert then explains how the requirements for unity and coherence in reports fit into his teaching goals in social studies. The boy again listens, and as soon as Robert finishes begins to argue that his teaching goals are wrong and unfair. Robert says, "You'll have to take your seat now. We can talk about this later if you don't understand." The boy returns reluctantly to his seat. In a few moments Robert stands and is about to begin a lesson with the class, when the boy returns, very close to tears. He insists that Robert is being unfair and hints that it's a personal thing and not an academic matter. The boy becomes very emotional and Robert again explains the purpose of the assignment and points out how the boy's paper does not fulfill it. He then sends the boy back to his seat, grumbling and desperately trying to hold back the tears. (After school Robert explained to the observer that the boy couldn't go home and face his parents without an A and that this was what he was upset about. He said, "The paper deserved a C and I'm sorry now I didn't give it that.") Robert says to the class, "Put the encyclopedias back." There is moaning and some children begin to write furiously while others load the books onto the carts. When all have been collected, six children roll the carts into the hall and race pell-mell for Ruth Tucker's fourth grade, where the books are now due. Robert asks, "Does anyone have answers for the challenges?" referring to the mathematics puzzles on the blackboard. A number of children volunteer answers and Robert writes the correct ones next to the puzzles. Then he says, "Now we will have science reports. Tommy." Tommy says, "I can't." Robert asks why and Tommy replies, "I need a battery." Robert asks, with a touch of sarcasm in his voice, "How long will it take you to get one?" Tommy replies sullenly, "I don't know." Robert nods to another boy and says, "Okay, Bob." Bob comes to the front of the room and rests a cross-sectional diagram of a bee on the chalk tray of the blackboard. He explains its various parts to the class and then asks for questions. A discussion develops about the functions of the different parts and their relations to each other. This leads to the topic of bee breeding, hatching, and the making of different kinds of bees; drones, queens, and so on. Robert quickly changes the subject to communication among bees and other kinds of insects and animals. The children begin feeding him questions to keep him on this diversion from the lesson. He knows what is happening and after a moment nods to a girl and says, "Okay, Donna." Donna comes to the front and places a cross-sectional diagram of a bird next to that of the bee. She also describes the parts to the class and then asks for questions. She and Robert answer the questions the children raise. When there seem to be no more questions Robert says, "Let me check and see if I missed anybody." He calls the names of children and the day they are to give reports.

Robert says he finds the attitudes of the children and the requirements of the curriculum the chief obstacles to realizing his teaching goals. The boy's attitude toward the grade on his social studies paper was typical of these children: "They are very oriented toward grades; they're oriented toward college, specifically. Their parents are pushing them to get high grades and they are pushing themselves so they can get into good colleges." He described this concern in the following interchange with an interviewer:

Interviewer: It's interesting to me that teachers from the lower grades report that the parents seem to be primarily concerned that their children get into Harvard, and what you say indicates that by the time they get to the sixth grade the *children* have internalized this goal.

Robert Paul: Oh, very definitely, very definitely. The kids don't seem to be aware of the intellectual prerequisites for entering a school like Harvard or MIT. They feel that if they can get As, no matter how they get them, that's all that's necessary. They don't seem to realize it isn't the only criterion for admission. But they are already concerned, they are all oriented toward going to college.

Robert feels that those children who are motivated to work in the sixth grade are motivated not to learn but to get the good grades which they and their parents see as essential for college admission. There is very little intellectual curiosity, very little desire to know for the sake of understanding things. This, of course, is a major disappointment for a man with his teaching goals.

In addition, Robert says, "I feel hampered in that I'm expected to teach the curriculum," which he feels has an adverse effect on the development of real intellectual interests and curiosity in the children. "For example," he says, "we're expected to cover the world outside North America in social studies. This means Europe, Africa, Asia, the Middle East, and Latin America, all in one year—can you imagine?" Robert went on to say that with such a required coverage the children could acquire no more than the most superficial understanding of these parts of the world. Each child is given a country of "his own" to report on, but Robert says, "This generally becomes a routine kind of encyclopedia copying" which holds no intrinsic interest.

Topics which would interest the sixth-grade children, Robert points out, he is forbidden to discuss in class. These are politics, religion, and sex. The discussion of real political issues is taboo in the public schools, Robert claims, and social studies has to be confined to descriptions of the geographies and economic products of countries. It is actually elementary economic geography, not "social studies" at all. The vague patriotic sentiments which characterize elementary school "current events" discussions have nothing to do with basic political issues, Robert feels, so he eschews such discussions altogether.

Any discussion of a religion-related issue, such as "Christians in many lands" is bound to bring complaints from parents, Robert says, who feel that their religion is being slighted or their rights are being violated. "In any discussion of religion," Robert says, "it always seems there is something to offend somebody, either Protestant, Catholic, or Jew." Even superficial references to religion, then, become taboo because of probable parental objection.

Any allusion to the processes of sexual reproduction in class will bring similar complaints from parents, Robert reported. This is why he cut off the discussion of the making of different kinds of bees. "I remember once," Robert said, "when I was very new, talking about how the guppies in the class fish tank got babies, and I had one mother in here nearly hysterical with fear lest her girl find out how children were conceived." This same mother, he went on to report with irony, was one of the main proponents of the sixth-grade graduation dance because she wanted her daughter to be popular with boys. "Primarily," Robert claimed, "these kids are socially oriented. They want to be popular with the opposite sex and their parents want them to be, too."

Robert summed up his frustrations in a discussion early in the year with the other male teacher, Johnny Long. Robert said, "Maybe we should be giving them 'education for life,' as John Dewey said, but we can't say anything about the important things in life, such as sexual reproduction or religion or politics." Johnny agreed, adding that regardless of "all the talk about teachers being professionals" they were "just civil servants who teach what the public wants us to—no more, no less." Robert felt that the combination of what might be called the required curriculum and the forbidden curriculum made elementary education superficial and unrealistic in the upper grades. By the time the children reach the sixth grade, it seems to him, they have little spontaneous interest left in learning and what remains or might be awakened is ruled out by the curriculum restrictions.

Robert, of course, finds his work fundamentally unsatisfying. In his own words, "I find my work not particularly fulfilling." He is studying at night working for a master's degree in psychology so he can become a school psychologist. When asked what he expects to gain from such a position, Robert replies that he would at least get the money and status he does not get as a man teaching elementary school. These are not all that important to him, he explains, saying, "I'd like to make more but we do fairly nicely on what I make," but their appeal is strong when combined with the lack of fulfillment from his present work. Principal Johnson fully expects Robert to leave. He said, "In two years Robert will be gone. But that will make it about as long as you can expect to keep someone like that in elementary school teaching." Johnson himself had gone from grade-school teaching into school administration.

Problems of Craftsman Teaching

Teachers with a craftsman orientation discover, after a number of years in the classroom, that they are unable to teach as they feel they should or to realize a significant portion of their educational goals. The teachers mention the attitudes of the children, the expectations of the parents, the requirements of the curriculum, and the large size of their classes as causes of their frustration. Briefly, instead of being able to teach individual children what they need to know and are ready to know about the world, the craftsman teachers, like the production teachers, find that their basic task is to teach classes of children the required school system curriculum.

In an attempt to conduct some individualized instruction, the lower-grade teachers who are experienced at their work create formal, bureaucratic organizations in their classrooms to control the behavior of the majority of the class while they teach individuals and small groups. Their entire relationship with the children becomes something different from what they originally sought. Instead of personal relations with individuals, they find they must establish impersonal relations with a group —which means that when they come to work with individuals and small groups, they interact as bureaucratic role-players, not as individuals. The end product of this interaction is something essentially alien to both parties, the mastery of the required curriculum.

The upper-grade craftsman teacher finds that by the time the children reach him they are conditioned bureaucratic role-players concerned with achieving the symbols of organizational success—high grades—and not curious, spontaneous seekers after knowledge and understanding. He is asked to teach these children a curriculum which he feels is superficial and unreal, being unrelated to important interests of the children or important things happening in the world. He is, in fact, explicitly forbidden to discuss such subjects, the most important of which would be politics, religion, and sexual reproduction. He and two of the lower-grade craftsman teachers have become successes in the school and school system terms and failures in their own terms, and all three plan to leave teaching.

The response to frustration for these teachers, then, is to move into other kinds of work or leave school altogether. Becky Yager and Robert Paul are going into advisory and specialist work and Hannah Gilbert has left education and will probably not return unless she finds a school in which she can do her kind of teaching. Only Alice Davis remains in the classroom and is happy with her work, finding it satisfies her need for the love of children. However, we can anticipate that she will soon have to create greater organization in her classroom, if only to avoid serious accidents. As she develops a formal classroom structure, her relations with the children will become more distant and much less satisfying for her.

Wilbur Wright School and the Brookview school system, on the other hand, seem outwardly to be places which would be particularly sympathetic to craftsman teaching. Principal Johnson, the school system administrators, and even the state commissioner of education, as was shown in the previous chapter, hold philosophies of education which imply the craftsman type of teaching. The discrepancy between the goals of the craftsman teachers and the demands of the classroom work is not the result of any ideological conflict with persons in power, whether they are in the state capital, the board of education office, or the principal's office at Wright School.[1]

The problems seem to stem from the demands of the organizational structure itself, reinforced by the demands of the neighborhood, community, and society the school ultimately serves. The school and the system are both complex bureaucratic organizations whose structure demands certain behavior for its most efficient functioning. These bureaucracies are accountable to the Brookview public and the Seaboard State government, both of which must approve and support their operation. The administrators, from principal to superintendent, must see that their organizations *are* acceptably accountable to the public and the state authority. The attitudes, values, and actions of the people in the neighborhood and the community with respect to the school are a function of their social position and their perceptions of the schools as public agencies and personal means for realizing their goals for their children. The following chapters will show how the combination of pressures from these different sources favors the success of a production orientation toward teaching rather than a craftsman orientation.

1. Superintendent of Schools Robert Nelson recommended Wright School to the researchers as the site for their study because of the "forward-looking, experimental attitude of the people there" and because, as was discovered in the course of the study, of his opinion that this was the best elementary school in the system, with the most intelligent and professional staff. Principal Johnson counted Becky, Hannah, and Robert as among his best teachers and relied heavily on them for helping him implement his educational program in the school.

3 The Production Teachers

The Production Orientation

Most of the teachers at the Wilbur Wright Elementary School have a production, rather than a craftsman orientation toward teaching. They conceive of their basic task as helping the children learn the skills and knowledge prescribed in the school system curriculum guides. A *Curriculum Guide* for each grade stipulates the subjects to be taught and the material to be covered in each, and gives recommended methods for teaching this material. The school system administration thus determines the amount and kind of reading, writing, spelling, arithmetic, social studies, science, and art which are to be mastered by the children at each elementary grade level. The production teacher takes these directives as the definition of her task, and seeks ways to transmit the required skills and knowledge to the children in her class. Whereas the craftsman teachers want to build a course of study around the interests of children to meet their individual learning needs, the production teachers want to transmit the required grade-level curriculum. This difference in orientation can be seen in the different kinds of informal, but work-oriented, discussions these teachers have. The craftsman teachers, when talking about their work, discuss what the children in their classes seem to be interested in and how these interests can be woven into a viable curriculum. The production teachers, on the other hand, share methods they have developed for getting the children to learn the material in the standard curriculum.

Most of the production teachers subscribe, at least verbally, to the official Wright School instructional philosophy of ignoring the formal grade-level divisions in the elementary-school curriculum and teaching each child as much as he can absorb of each subject during each year. Since this is nominally the working goal of each teacher, the fact that good students will be working a year or even two ahead of their formal grade level in some subjects does not present a problem, for presumably the teacher they have the next year will take them on from whatever point they have reached. Each teacher, under this system, must be ready to teach on a wide range of grade levels. In the fourth grade, for example, a teacher will probably have children reading or doing arithmetic on second- through seventh-grade levels. She must stock teaching materials from all of these grades and be ready to give instruction on each level.

This scaling of the required curriculum to what seem to be the abilities of the individual children is "individualized teaching" as defined by the production-oriented teachers. They are trying to reach the children "as individuals," they say, in order to assess their level of achievement and their learning potential, so they can minister to their "learning needs," defined as the amount of the standard elementary-school curriculum they are capable of mastering at this point in their lives. Efficiency can be said to be the goal of the production teachers, especially those who subscribe to the official Wright School philosophy, for they are committed to helping the children learn the standardized school curriculum as fast as they can.

The goals of the production teachers are congruent with the structure of the Brookview educational bureaucracy, and not at variance with it, as are the goals of the craftsman teachers, because the production teachers seek to efficiently administer the given school system curriculum. They can be expected to experience less organizationally generated difficulty in their work, and certainly to avoid altogether the fundamental contradiction between structure and goals which is experienced by the craftsman teachers. The production teachers who subscribe to the Wright School philosophy, of teaching each child as much of the curriculum as he can absorb during the year, which most do at least verbally, can also see themselves as engaging in the "individualized education" advocated in the rhetoric of the modern educators from their instructors in college to their superintendent in Brookview and their principal at Wright School. The production teachers do not experience the qualitative difference between their kind of individualized instruction, which involves taking each child through the prescribed educational program at his own pace, and the individualized education attempted by the craftsman teachers, which involves building the curriculum itself out of the current interests of the children.

The production teachers' version of individualized instruction does not meet a fundamental structural contradiction within the school system, as does that of the craftsman teachers, but they nevertheless encounter problems in its implementation. These are problems of learning and limitations of time, knowledge, and skill on the part of the teacher. Such problems, as we will see, reflect limitations of the experience and training of the faculty, and the financing and organization of education in Brookview, but no fundamental contradictions between teachers' goals and organizational structure.

The simplest set of practical problems is found in the implementation of the Wright School instructional philosophy by inexperienced teachers. Yvonne Valuzzi, a new third-grade teacher just out of college, described some of the problems she encountered in her first few months at Wright School. She said,

I go along with the philosophy, of course, of developing each child individually and trying to help them attain the most they can. I've found more what that means since I've been teaching, I think, than all the times I said it, and heard it said, in teachers college. [Asked, "What have you found it means?"] Well, for example, it means that you have to learn not to get disturbed if all the children can't do exactly the same thing, and help them to be satisfied that some can't achieve the same as others. Then you have to find things for all of them to do (according to their ability) instead of finding one thing for all of them to do. And some finish their work long before others, and of course they just can't sit idle, they should be doing something worthwhile. This is one of the things that gave me a lot of trouble because when I went to school it was not like this, if you finished first, you sat and waited for everybody. And I wasn't prepared for this in teachers college either.

Yvonne, like other teachers in her position, has discovered that she must get used to having children in her room working on many different levels, at least in their basic subjects. She must learn to teach on these levels, which may range over four grades in subjects like reading and arithmetic. She must also console the children who are not learning as rapidly as others to be satisfied with the level of achievement they can obtain. Finally, she must keep the fast learners working on "something worthwhile" and not just filling in their time with busywork. All these skills a new teacher with a production orientation must learn if she is serious about implementing the Wright School "philosophy" of instruction.

An older, experienced second-grade teacher, Sylvia Baxter, commented on the importance of individual attention to children in carrying out the goals of the production teacher; that is, seeing that the children mastered the prescribed academic curriculum. She said,

I really feel that I have no right to be here in the classroom unless I give every child time every day to work with me. I know that with these little seven-year-olds if I don't give them some time to read with me and to work with me on the workbook or on written materials every day, that child is going to slip back because they don't learn any way except repetition. And if there's too long a break between repeating you lose them. I know that you can bring up most any child, even of dull-normal level, with constant work like this, but you can't do it with a little bit [of attention] here and a little bit there. So I feel that it's my duty to see that these children get as much of my time as they can, and if I'm not reaching them one way, I feel I should sit down and study it and try a new way to put it across, to make what I'm trying to teach them stick, to help them with retention. They just have to repeat and repeat, and it has to be given to them so they want to remember, or they don't have it.

Mastery of the standard curriculum, Sylvia is saying here, involves the traditional kind of rote learning in which children are drilled in their lessons—"they just have to repeat and repeat"—until they remember the material they are supposed to learn. The production orientation toward teaching assumes that the material to be learned is external and foreign to the children, so that ways must be found to force or induce them to learn it. Sylvia uses constant repetition to induce mastery of the curriculum material while, as she suggests in her last statement, searching for ways to "give" the academic material to the children so they will "want" to learn it. This latter problem is a theme which appears over and over again in the discussions of the production teachers, and it is usually phrased as the problem of how to "motivate" the children to learn the required academic material; how to find ways of getting them to "want" to learn what they "must" learn. This problem is of course inherent in an educational program which is imposed upon children from the outside rather than being developed through their own interests.

The production teachers feel that their work would be accomplished more efficiently if the children's spontaneous interests could be tapped as a potent source of motivation. They consult education journals for new ways to "motivate children to learn" and discuss among themselves and with the special teachers different ways of getting children interested in required curriculum. The problem does not occur in this form for the craftsman teachers, of course, because they are attempting to fashion their very curriculums out of the interests of the children. The production teachers must seek artificial ways of relating learning to the children's interests because the curriculum has not been developed out of these interests in the first place.

Wendy Thomas, a young, experienced, and very serious first-grade teacher with a production orientation discussed a number of problems she had encountered in implementing her goals as a teacher. She said she was "dedicated to the Wright School philosophy: We take a child from where he is when he comes into our room and take him as far as he can go in all the subjects while we have him," and went on to list the problems she had to cope with in her teaching:

This is my actual goal. In reality I'm pretty sure I don't always accomplish it, because to really accomplish a goal like that you have to have much more individual attention than we are able to give in class. This year is the smallest class I've ever had, twenty-five, and I think even this, for kindergarten and first grade, is too many to be able to follow through on a goal like taking the child from where he is to where he can go. What we, what I, probably end up doing is taking him from where he is when he comes to me to as far as my time will allow and as far as his time will allow within a class.

Wendy has made a realistic readjustment of her goals according to the limited amount of time she has to spend with each child. There is never enough time in a year, Wendy thinks, to get to know each child in the class well enough to ascertain all his potentialities for learning, let alone help him actually fulfill these. Wendy and the teachers like her know that it is necessary to understand children emotionally as well as intellectually in order to help them learn to their fullest capacity. She feels that she always needs "more time to get to know a child, to know what he is feeling" in order to help him with his learning. Summing up her feelings about teaching, Wendy says, "I get a strong sense of frustration sometimes knowing I'll never be able to reach all the children the way I feel I ought to."

Wendy has taught third and sixth grade and has been a perceptive observer of children in these classrooms. She has noted a growing discrepancy, as children move through the elementary grades, between their potentialities and their accomplishments. There is a gap, she feels, between ability and accomplishment which widens each year because each teacher is unable to give sufficient individual attention. Teachers lack the time, and sometimes the skills, to discover each child's full potential for learning and guide him individually to its realization. Because of this, Wendy feels, children gradually lose genuine interest in learning. The spontaneity and enthusiasm which characterize the children's discovery of themselves and the world in the first grade diminish year by year and are gradually replaced by stereotyped responses to the school situation. By the time children reach the sixth grade, spontaneous interest has been completely replaced by a desire to simply give the teacher what they think she wants, Wendy claims. This, she feels, is the ultimate consequences of there being insufficient time for teachers to come to know their children well.

This loss of spontaneity and genuine interest in schoolwork over the years was remarked upon by many educators in Brookview, including curriculum coordinator Saul Levine, who also attributed it to aspects of the school program. The production orientation itself undoubtedly contributes to this growing estrangement of the children from the subject matter they must learn. The production teachers are attempting to inculcate the prescribed school system curriculum into all the children as efficiently as possible. Teachers like Wendy Thomas seek to know the children as individuals so as to find more effective ways of inducing them to learn the standard curriculum materials. They are not, as the craftsman teachers are, trying to understand the children in order to develop a program of learning from their spontaneous interests. Thus it is probably not just years of experience with teachers who do not have sufficient time to get to know them personally which alienates children from schoolwork, but perhaps even more important, the cumulative experiences of years of external learning tasks, quite foreign to the children's genuine interests.

There are a few production-oriented teachers at Wright School who do not subscribe to the school's official instructional philosophy. These teachers conceive of their task as teaching only the material assigned to their grade in the school system curriculum guides. Irene Goodenough, for example, said her goal was "just trying to get them to learn everything they should know in the third grade." Fifth-grade teacher Dorothy Jones saw her task similarly as administering the fifth-grade curriculum to the children. She said,

My job is to see that these children learn what they should know in the fifth grade. To me this is the prime purpose of my work. If these children can understand each grade's work as they go along, and build a background for further learning, it seems this is particularly important because there is so much pressure in our society at this time for going on to college. . . . And I think if you can motivate children to want to learn so that they can learn some of these things themselves, then when they get to college they're going to be so much better off. . . . I think that if you can motivate children to want to learn you have accomplished your prime purpose.

The problem of "motivating" the children to learn the prescribed subject matter is seen as central to the long-range tasks of the educational system, in an implicit recognition of the basically alien nature of the curriculum.

Joan Dexter is the teacher with the longest experience in education. She is just a few years from retirement, and she sees her task as a teacher quite clearly and simply. When asked her philosophy of education she replied, "That's simple; I learn 'em." Asked further what it was she "learned 'em" Joan replied,

Well, in the skills, as far as subject matter is concerned, I want them to know what they should know at the end of the sixth grade. As far as arithmetic is concerned, they should know addition, subtraction, multiplication, division, and fractions and decimals and be able to do problems with these. And in reading I think I should try to get them all up to at least a 6.1 level. And in spelling, they should be able to spell the most commonly used words. As far as the other subjects are concerned, I hope I am able to teach them how to study, and then to try to have them be happy and enjoy life and be considerate, in other words, to get along with people.

Politeness, courtesy, and "getting along with others" were mentioned as important goals by a number of teachers with the pro-

duction orientation. They basically involve problems of classroom management—of disciplining children to behave as they
are expected to in class. Because the subject matter is external
to the children, for the most part not coming from any interest
of their own, all these teachers have to be concerned with
developing social control mechanisms in the classroom. Here,
as with instruction itself, they feel that internalized mechanisms
of social control will be far more efficient than a constant application of external constraints.

In contrast to the craftsman teachers, the production
teachers seem to face a set of problems for which adequate
solutions can be found during the course of a teaching career.
This is so because their goals as teachers are basically congruent with the requirements of the educational bureaucracy,
not at fundamental variance as are the goals of the craftsman
teachers. Production teachers who take seriously the Wright
School philosophy of instruction and try to teach each child
the curriculum according to his ability to absorb it will find
themselves frustrated by the lack of time to get to know each
child well and teach him individually. These teachers can,
however, readjust their goals within the system, as Wendy
Thomas has, to being satisfied with giving as much individual
attention as they can in the time they have. Ultimately they
need not feel guilty about this compromise, because it is made
necessary by the limitations of the system, not by their own
limitations as teachers. They can simply say they are assigned
too many children to accomplish the goal held up for them,
and that they do their best within the organizational limitations on their work.

The production teachers can also adjust to their working
situation by adopting the still-respectable goal of teaching the
curriculum of their grade. Teachers like Dorothy Jones can
adopt the comfortable rationale for such a goal, saying that if
the children learn what they are supposed to in each grade
throughout school they will be able to get into college, which
for them is a definition of success in the school system. This
definition of educational success is shared by most of the
Brookview parents, and so the orientation of these teachers

is compatible with some of the desires and expectations of the parents of their pupils. Thus, even though they do not subscribe to the official philosophy of Wright School, these teachers hold educational goals which do find support in the community.

All the production teachers must face the problem of loss of interest and spontaneity as the children move, year by year, through the prescribed curriculum. They must constantly work out solutions to the problems of motivation and discipline in the classroom, and they seek artificial ways to use the children's spontaneous interests as motivating forces in learning. Entire technologies, from the simplest gimmicks to the most elaborate programs, are devised by the classroom teachers and the helping teachers for "stimulating children's interest" in the prescribed work. At the same time, obedience to authority and conformity to authoritatively imposed routines are used as the chief devices for maintaining order. The suburban, middle-class children of Brookview can be relied upon to submit to discipline imposed by strong authority emanating from a legitimate source, and most will do their lessons if only because it is required by school and home authority. This does not mean, as will be seen later, that they submit to the discipline of the classroom and the curriculum without resistance or rebellion. Both of these forms of protest are regular occurrences in Wright School classrooms. Such is bound to be the case when the fundamental task at hand is alien to the genuine interests of the participants.

Production Teaching in the Classroom
Teachers with a production orientation eventually seem to work out ways of enforcing the standard curriculum which involve about half of their classes in active participation and the remainder in passive acquiescence to schoolwork. An educator observing their classrooms would say they are "reaching" or "involving" or "motivating" about half the children while they don't seem to "be getting through" to the others. Those who exercise strong authority manage to keep all the children under control, and so children who are not "involved in learning" are at least not disruptive to the class; they become passive

recipients of the lessons who manage to master enough of the material to avoid serious sanctions. There are, of course, a few children in more or less permanent active rebellion against both curriculum and the school authority, and they become infamous as the school "problem children" who can be counted upon to disturb teacher-imposed discipline in any class. These responses to educational processing will be examined in a later chapter. Here we shall look briefly into some classrooms to see just how production teaching is carried on and observe some of the children's responses.

Wendy Thomas's First Grade: A Morning in the Middle of December. The children are seated at their desks looking at their arithmetic books while Wendy gives a lesson from the front of the room. Half of the twenty or so children turn to watch as the visitor enters and continue to be distracted by his presence even though he takes a chair at the back of the room near the door. After a few minutes more of the lesson Wendy says, "Put your books away, and paper helpers pass out work paper," and two girls pass out paper to the children at their desks. Wendy says, "First reading group please," and six children come to the front and sit in a semicircle of chairs. They take turns reading to Wendy, who sits in a chair facing them and the classroom behind them. She calls the names of children who talk or otherwise make disturbances while the reading lesson is in progress. The children at their desks are copying letters from a writing book. In about ten minutes the reading group disperses and two little girls, one on each side of the room, make a noise getting out of their chairs. Wendy asks them what they want, and they look at each other and look down at their desks. One mumbles, "She always beats me to the chair." Wendy asks why they race for the chair in the reading circle and neither answers. A third child volunteers that the person who sits in that chair gets to distribute the readers to the group (it is the chair next to the bookshelves under the blackboard). Wendy says "Yes, that's what I thought, and that's why I have put the books on your seats."

Various kinds and degrees of children's involvement in school activities are evident in this observation. It is apparent from the reaction to the visitor that only half the class is involved in the arithmetic lesson that is in progress when he enters. (Reaction to a visitor, the degree to which his presence disturbs children or distracts them is, as was pointed out in the last chapter, a reliable measure of the degree of involvement of children in their classroom activity, the strength of teacher disciplinary control, or both.) Here, as in a number of production classrooms, the visitor, making himself as inconspicuous as possible and already a known figure in the school, seriously distracts a good portion of a lower-grade class being led in a routine lesson by the teacher. Half the class, on the other hand, remains unaffected, either continuing to pay attention to the lesson or following their own private distractions. Two girls are involved very strongly in a contest of their own, trying to acquire the role of book distributor for their reading group.

The kinds of involvement which persist to the end of the year are illustrated in the following observation of Wendy's class.

Wendy Thomas's First Grade: Late Afternoon in Early June. The children are at their desks, apparently engaged in "free time" activity. Some work with clay, others build with blocks, a few color with crayons, and some play with games and small toys. Wendy is in the back of the room putting reading books back on their shelves and generally straightening up for closing. She says, "You have five minutes to get ready." Children begin to put away the things they are working and playing with, either on the shelves or in storage cabinets. Most of them seem to have been modeling in clay, making vague resemblances of animals they saw on a recent trip to the Metropolitan City Zoo. A couple of children ask Wendy, "Can we play bingo?" She asks the class, "How many want to play bingo?" Half of the twenty or so children present raise their hands or call out, "Me!" Wendy tells them to sit in the two rows of desks on the right side of the room, and asks the children sitting there to change their places. There is some noise and grumbling from those being displaced by the bingo players. They go and wander around the left side of the room aimlessly.

Wendy tells them to "get a book or a toy or a game and work at a desk for the rest of the time." This turns out to be a very complex and confusing operation, with children going all over the room looking for things, trying to decide what they want from the shelves at the back of the room, which are cluttered with all sorts of games and play materials. Some are still confused and do not know why they are being displaced from their desks or what they are expected to do.

Wendy gives the bingo cards to a girl. They contain first-grade reading words and are, of course, an instructional device, or "teaching aid." The girl distributes the cards to the players and begins reading off the words. The children move from their first to their second bingo game in total absorption. They are completely caught up in the game. The boys have been pitted against the girls, and all seem bent on winning. Wendy has to call to order a number of the other children, who are supposed to be playing by themselves, but never needs to say a word to the bingo players. The bingo game moves into the third round and Wendy continues to neaten the room and try to keep the other children in order. She says to them, when they are making noise or running around the room, "What are you doing?" and "What are you supposed to be doing?" and "Well, do it at your desk please." Wendy tells the bingo group, "Time for one more game," and the children moan. She says to the visitor, "They are a good group. They function on their own. That's the way they should by this time of the year. When they work like this, I feel I have accomplished what I want. They have achieved some measure of independence." When she calls an end to the bingo game the girls shout in joy, "We won! We won!" and the boys loudly protest the ending of the game.

Here it can be seen that the "independence" which Wendy feels the children have achieved by this time of the year is the ability to administer their own learning. The bingo players have adopted one of the devices invented for involving children in their learning as a game of their own, and put themselves through this learning experience with great enthusiasm and concentration. The common cultural device of team competition has been employed in this game to heighten interest, and about half the children in the class are able to become involved in this.

One way to get the children to absorb the required subject matter, then, is to use technologies such as this which are devised by educators and psychologists on the basis of conceptions of the "mental capacities" of children of various ages and the "natural interests" of children in our society in general. A favorite technique is the one used in Wendy's room of connecting the curriculum with the children's play world, using toys, games, and other "children's things" as teaching devices. Games, toys, and other play materials are in evidence in the lower-grade classrooms in Wright School, and some parents complain that "all they ever do at that school is play." We have seen here, however, that these are very much a part of production-oriented teaching, being used both as teaching devices and as social control mechanisms in these classrooms.

A more elaborate device for eliciting children's interest in schoolwork and their involvement in the subject matter is the instructional unit, in which the academic skills are taught as part of a larger unit of study organized around some topic such as the life of the American Indians. The following observation from a third grade illustrates this.

Nancy Hoover's Third Grade: Late in January. This room is one of the most active in the school right now. The bulletin board across the back wall is covered with a huge composite mural depicting the lives of four types of American Indians, and this is surrounded with pinned-up children's book reports with brightly crayoned covers. The shelf under this bulletin board, also running the length of the room, is lined with imitation Indian craft work, including painted pottery and basketry made by the children. Along the wall under the windows is a long table covered with materials for making Indian musical instruments, such as rattles, shakers, and drums. Next to this table is one of the large rolling carts used by the helping teachers to take these materials from room to room. It is full of materials for making the instruments. The children are at their desks working in their arithmetic books. Nancy shows the visitor the Indian work with obvious pride. She feels the children have done a wonderful job on this unit. "Of course," she says, "Agnes and Edith [the art and music helping teachers] have shown us how to make these things." The children have been allowed to choose which of the four Indian groups they would study, and then have done their book reports and made handicrafts and musical instruments used by its people.

Some children are doing arithmetic in their books, some are talking, others are walking around the room. Nancy comes to the front and says, "All right, everyone, put your books away [there are moans from some, who apparently haven't finished] and we'll review for our test." Nancy pulls her chair to the center of the front, sits, and begins drilling the children on questions about their Indian unit. She asks, "What kind of house did the Plains Indians live in?" and four or five children throw their hands in the air to be called on, some straining and making "ou, ou" sounds in order to attract her attention. A girl who is called on says, "The Plains Indians lived in tepees," and smiles, seeming very smug and pleased with herself. Nancy says, "Very good" and goes on to other questions such as, "Where do the Pueblo Indians live?" The children always look very pleased with themselves after answering a question, and about half of them are playing this question and answer game. All the questions are cut-and-dried "facts" and the children seem more pleased with being called on and showing off before the class than with knowing the answers. A couple of children bring up things from books they have read, but apparently these aren't going to be on their test, and Nancy ignores them. In fact, she seems annoyed at being interrupted in the question-and-answer routine. Children who aren't participating in the answering—about half the class—look at books on their desks, whisper to one another, or just look absently around the room, obviously bored and restless.

The class becomes somewhat noisy with the talking and movement of the uninterested children and the efforts of the others to be called upon, and after ten minutes Nancy rises and says, "All right, that's enough. Now finish your work, then finish your instruments." Some children pull books and papers from their desks and set to work and others go immediately to the big metal cart and get materials for making their instruments. These are, for the most part, children who were participating in answering questions just previously. They seem to be the ones really involved in the Indian unit.

Art, social studies, music, reading, and even science have been combined in this unit of study of the American Indian to make these subjects more interesting to the children and thereby motivate their learning. This sort of program is considered rather advanced for a production-oriented teacher. Even so, it is obvious that only about half the children are actively involved in the unit, and an important part of this involvement is apparently just identification with schoolwork generally and the desire to excel at it and show off to their fellow pupils. These children seem interested in excelling regardless of the content of the lesson, since they respond to both the dry "factual" material and the more "creative" material, whereas the other half of the class seems uninterested in both these aspects of the Indian unit. The actively participating children seem to identify with the role of pupil rather than being motivated by the subject matter itself. They will, in a literal sense, perform the acts required by the pupil role without, it seems, really caring about the material of the curriculum.

The ersatz enthusiasm displayed so conspicuously by the children identifying with the pupil role certainly in part reflects the fact that the subject matter, even though presented in the form of an interest-eliciting unit, remains alien to them. The "creative work" on the handicrafts and musical instruments, for example, has been created, but by the art and music teachers, not by the children. Out of their knowledge and experience these women have developed Indian products which can be imitated by the children from materials they supply. The objects the children make are created by them only in the sense of actual construction. The creative act came previously in the teachers' (or their teachers') invention of these imitation Indian products and the methods for building them.

Even in a unit program that involves such a wide variety of activities, teachers like Nancy are ultimately concerned that the children learn simple memorized material to give back on a test of the most unimaginative kind—the kind of information which could have been gotten from the dullest text or reference book. The elaborate Indian unit with all its musical and artistic activities has really been a device for inducing children to learn a certain set of subjects, and at the end it is these subjects they must give back on their examinations.

A more complex set of pupil responses to the production-organized classroom is indicated in the following observation from Nancy's class later in the year.

Nancy Hoover's Third Grade: Early June. Nancy is seated in the center of the front of the room reading to the class from a book about Brookview. Each child has a copy of the book on his desk. Some look at the book, some look at Nancy, others gaze around the room looking out the window or at the visitor, who sits in the back. Nancy adds to the information in the book as she reads, and children occasionally ask questions or add comments. They look very pleased with themselves each time they do this. The children's questions gradually move further and further from the topic, and Nancy concludes the lesson, telling them to "think about some questions about Brookview over the weekend." She then says, "Now we'll have a seventh-inning break and play Simon Says." The children all stand and begin talking. "I want this talking stopped," Nancy snaps. When the last child is out in Simon Says, Nancy says, "Now we're going to have a science report." A number of children cry, "Oh, oh" with great insistence and four or five rush to her desk. Six others stand by their own desks waving their hands in the air and jumping up and down. Nancy walks past all of them to the back of the room where she stands in silence among the children pleading, "Please teacher, can I do my report now?" She says, "I'm waiting for you to be seated." When they are she calls on a girl who goes to the front and reads a short report on snakes. Nancy asks her for definitions of terms she uses, such as forked tongue. Half the children are looking at the reader; the rest look at their desks, out the window, at the teacher, or at the visitor. Few seem to be paying attention to what the child who was finally chosen to report is saying. Even before she is finished speaking, half a dozen children have their hands in the air, trying to be the first to be called on to make comments or ask questions. When they are called on, their comments and questions are only slightly related to the topic of the paper. They seem, in fact, hardly interested in the topic, but rather in being given the chance to say something. Only about half the class is playing this attention-getting game. The rest are doing things at their desks or looking dully around the room or out the window. A number yawn and look at the clock. It is close to dismissal time. Two girls return to the room and Nancy asks them with some sarcasm, "Did you have a good time?" One looks sheepish, the other defiant, and the latter comes up to Nancy and demands to know what the class is doing. They have been out of the room at least since the visitor arrived.

Here again the behavior of the participating children seems to involve attempts to call attention to themselves rather than participate in any intelligent discussion of the subject matter. In the case of the report, they may not even pay attention to what is being said, but simply wait until the presentation is almost over and then throw their hands in the air and make the pleading "ou, ou" sound indicating that they want to be recognized. At least half the class will not even bother to try to participate, but simply sit out the lesson in silence unless it becomes evident that the teacher is looking for comments from all the children, in which case they will allow themselves to be drawn reluctantly into the recognition game. A few others will drop out altogether and avoid the lesson by finding a way to absent themselves from the room. Identification with the role of pupil (not with the subject matter of the curriculum), acquiescence to classroom procedures and reluctant participation when called upon, and outright rejection of the classroom situation seem to be alternative responses of children to their processing in production-oriented classrooms.

This variation in response can be held to a minimum, at least to external appearances, by a thoroughgoing regimentation of the elementary-school classroom. Third-grade teacher Irene Goodenough uses the curriculum to achieve total social control in her classroom to the extent that all students at least appear to spend the entire school day on assigned work. Some excerpts from a day in Irene's room show how she creates this control of the situation.

Irene Goodenough's Third Grade: Early June. When the 8:45 bell rings for school to begin, Irene says, "All right, let's take our seats," and walks to the back of her classroom. Most of the children are already at their desks, and the rest sit down. A girl goes to the front of the room and reads a child's name from a list in a lower corner of the blackboard. This boy comes forward and leads the class in the Lord's Prayer. When he is finished, the girl reads the next name, and this child comes forward and reads a few verses from the Old Testament. When this is done the third name is read, and this child leads the class in the Pledge of Allegiance to the Flag. Irene asks the girl what song she wants, and the reply is "America." Irene plays this and three other songs the class knows on the piano and the class sings them. Following the songs, the girl in charge commands, "First table, come front!" and the children sitting in the first row of desks come to the front of the room. Each in turn shows something to the class and says something about it. Some have brought toys and books from home, others read short poems, some show pictures they have cut from magazines, and some tell recent experiences they have had. This is continued until every one of the thirty or more children has said something to the class.

At 9:15 Irene comes to the front of the room and begins to explain the day's assignment on the blackboard. The entire board is covered with this material. Irene begins explaining the arithmetic problems which are written out on the board. The children ask a few questions and then she goes on to the reading assignment, then the spelling assignment, then writing for the day, and finally a phonics workbook assignment. Then there are two listings under "work for after you finish," a social studies project and a science project. Irene clarifies the written instructions after having a child read them from the board, and then asks for questions in each of these areas. She orders one of the girls to pass out the arithmetic paper, and the children all begin work as soon as they have a sheet.

At 9:25 six children carry their chairs to a place in the back of the room and arrange them in a semicircle around an empty chair there. Irene sits in this chair and the children read to her, one by one, from their books. There is absolute silence elsewhere in the room, and all the other children are bent over the work at their desks.

Irene's class continues to function with this perfect precision and quiet throughout the day. Recess is carried off as smoothly as morning exercises, with a boy in charge of each of four class teams which have their games for the day in a notebook kept by the captain. Returning after lunch the children set to work again at their desks, and Irene meets with more reading groups. By the middle of the afternoon she feels it necessary to ask for quiet in the room, but no noise has ever become noticeable to the observer. No more than two children are allowed to be out of their seats at one time, and Irene only finds it necessary to call this rule to the attention of the class two or three times in the middle of the afternoon. Children leave to go to the toilets by signing out on a sheet on the teacher's desk. Only one boy and one girl are allowed out at a time, and many children wait patiently at their desks for a chance to sign out. Toward the end of the afternoon Irene checks the children's morning work. On this particular day this procedure was rather revealing.

Irene has checked the children's arithmetic and writing by 2:30 and says, "All right, now we'll check phonics." A number of children volunteer answers to the exercises they have been assigned in their workbooks. When called on they come to the front of the room and read their answers. The situation rapidly becomes very confused. It is apparent that the children have not understood this material, which they have been working at a good part of the afternoon. Those who volunteer and come to the front usually do not have the correct answers. Children in their seats call out their answers. There is apparently little relation between knowing the answer and volunteering to give it. Children who volunteer as often as not do not have an answer and it is given by another child or by Irene. But the children are very confused because most have few if any correct answers and they cannot understand what they have done wrong. Irene, after explaining the assignment all over again, says, "Those who haven't finished their phonics do them tonight and bring them in tomorrow."

Here, as in Nancy Hoover's room, there is evidence that volunteering has little relation to being able to do the work, and seems to be a bid for recognition from the teacher and the class. More serious, as a comment on this kind of classroom, is the fact that all the children in the class spent part of their day on an assignment that few if any of them understood. They applied themselves diligently to work which made no sense whatever to them simply because it was authoritatively imposed. The children are totally controlled here by the curriculum enforced by the teacher's classroom organization, even when the work is meaningless to them.

Irene's classroom is like an automated assembly line in which the behavior of each component is programmed beforehand and the outcome is generally predictable. All the children are put through the same material at the same pace (except for the work in the different reading groups, some of which are more advanced than others) and are expected to produce identical products at the end of the day. On the particular day reported here it can be said that the machine was inadequately programmed. However—and this is the important point about this kind of programmed classroom—the children kept at their task even when it made no sense because of incorrect instruction, simply because this was part of the assignment authoritatively given them. Irene's class shows the kind of total control possible with the production orientation toward teaching.

Training for Pupil Roles in Production Classrooms
The fourth grade at Wright School marks an important transition point in school experience for the children. Fourth, fifth, and sixth grades are considered the "upper grades" of the elementary school, while first, second, and third are the "lower grades." At the beginning of the upper grades children are expected to start learning to teach themselves the curriculum and to rely less on a direct relationship with the teacher to

mediate this learning. Fourth grade concentrates on teaching the children a new kind of educational procedure: they are instructed in the use of reference materials and libraries, in the school and in the community, and given assignments to carry out "on their own" through research in the source materials. All the fourth grade teachers reported that their primary goal was helping the children become capable of "independent work" during the year. This is the only grade in which the teachers see their primary goal as procedural rather than substantive; that is, as teaching a certain kind of learning behavior rather than a certain portion of the subject matter. The fourth-grade teachers are of course responsible for teaching the material assigned to this grade in the curriculum, but they all see the mastery of this subject matter as secondary to learning the new method of self-instruction.

The fourth grade transition from child-in-the-classroom to self-guided learner is a result of the demands of the Brookview educational program for the elementary schools. Children in the upper elementary grades are expected to carry out research projects as a major portion of their classroom work. As the first class in which children experience this demand, the fourth grade naturally gets the task of teaching children how to carry out this required independent work. The fourth-grade teachers at Wright School have not, so far as can be determined, gotten together and decided in concert that teaching children to work on their own is their main task. Each seems to have arrived at this definition of her work from the requirements of the Brookview program. Fourth grade is where the children have to begin learning based on their own research work, so fourth-grade teachers must instruct them in research procedures. Karen Olsen expressed this orientation of the fourth-grade teachers in this way:

Well, number one, you're trying to teach children how to find things out; where to go when they have something they want to find an answer to. You want to teach them certain fundamentals in reading and arithmetic, but I think the most important thing is to get them to be wondering why things are happening, and trying to understand why they're happening. I don't like stuffing facts into children and making them repeat them back to me. I'd much rather have them know where they can find the answer to something I ask and to be able to go and find it, than to have it on the tip of their tongue and spit it back to me.

Here Karen clearly reveals the nature of the "independent learning" which the fourth-grade teachers are training the children for: it consists basically of being able to find on their own the information required in the curriculum. This kind of learning is well within the production teacher's orientation, as it is concerned with training the children to master the assigned curriculum material on their own.

Fourth-grade teacher Lois Madden was the prime mover in establishing the central library at Wright School, so that children in her class could have access to source materials beyond those which could be purchased on her classroom book budget. Describing her teaching goals she said, "I am more concerned about developing good study skills than with the academic knowledge—that can come later." She said that when children come to her they "haven't learned yet how to move along the tracks independently, and this is the important thing to develop at this level, which I think is a very crucial stage in their development." Lois described her teaching program for this stage of development in this way:

The on-grade student has learned 90 percent of the basic skills when he comes to the fourth grade. In fourth grade we're strengthening these skills and extending them, and this they can teach themselves. I develop a plan, give them a framework, and then try to get them working independently in it. My better students start right off with independent work in reading, and slowly, very slowly, I get the rest working this way. They don't gather around "mamma hen" and perform for her like they do in the lower grades. I assign them projects which they do in the library or with our library here in the room and then report on to the rest of the class. It's a long time [during the year] before they are really moving ahead on their own, functioning independently, but there are days beginning in January or February when my class is rolling along and where I do very little teaching orally, where the children are teaching themselves, really, on their various levels.

Lois sees self-teaching of the subjects required by the curriculum or assigned by the teacher as the goal of her work with children in the fourth grade.

The "weaning" process which begins in the fourth grade with training the children in self-administration of the curriculum may help account for the increased disaffection from school at this point which was noted by a number of the Brookview educators. Interaction between the children and the teacher is gradually being replaced by a direct relation of the children to academic research material, with the teacher facilitating this relationship from the outside. In this grade, increased social distance in the basic classroom relationship is added to the absence of intrinsic interest in the subject matter to create something close to a totally alienating situation for the children. The curriculum does not provide a source of identification, and performance for immediate recognition and acceptance by the teacher is no longer possible. Adult recognition now comes through the longer and more difficult process of thorough research and good report writing, and it is given in more adult terms of praise for a job well done and less in terms of the teacher's acceptance of the pupils as good children.

The fourth-grade teachers describe their good pupils as those who learn to carry out their work on their own and their excellent pupils as those who seek work beyond that assigned to the class. Describing some of her good pupils, Charlotte Robinson said,

They love their research work. They had to make a bibliography for me in this last social studies unit. Some of them used ten or eleven books, and this I feel is terrific for the fourth grade; that they didn't take one encyclopedia and copy everything out of it. And they'll compare. They'll say, "How come this encyclopedia gives this height for this mountain, and this one gives another height?" Things like this. I feel that this is very good.

Vera Swartz described the kind of pupil she considers to be exceptional:

Quite often, around the middle of the year, they will come to me and say, "Can I do a report on such-and-such"—which is not something I assigned. I mean this is extra work that they want to do on their own. Seeing them go ahead on their own like that, you feel that you've really accomplished something with them.

"Problem children," on the other hand, are seen as those who never take up working on their own but have to have the curriculum administered to them by the teacher throughout the year, and are constantly demanding her personal attention, often by "acting up" in the classroom. Such pupils are referred to as "childish" by these teachers, and they seek the help of the school psychologist and the principal in finding ways to control and teach them. Fourth grade might be characterized as the year in which the term "childish" comes to be employed to describe behavior considered undesirable by teachers.

Production Teaching in the Upper Grades

The work the children carry on in the classrooms of the upper-grade production-oriented teachers is for the most part prescribed in the school system curriculum. This means that regardless of whether they are working under the direct supervision of the teacher or "independently" under her indirect guidance, they are engaged in tasks basically foreign to their own interests and desires, to which they must be disciplined by the teacher and for which they must be motivated to work. The fourth-, fifth-, and sixth-grade teachers face this task of enforcing the curriculum, regardless of the methods they use to present the required subject matter. Upper-grade production teachers, as we have already seen, consider their most important tasks as motivating children to want to learn and teaching them how to get along smoothly with one another—which also means obeying the teacher and conforming to classroom routines. Fifth-grade teacher Dorothy Jones said that the "prime purpose" of her work was "to see that these children learn what they should know in the fifth grade" and was of the opinion that "if you can motivate children to want to learn you have accomplished your prime purpose." Sixth-grade teacher Joan Dexter said she wanted the children in her class "to know what they should know at the end of the sixth grade" and hoped to teach the children how to be "happy and enjoy life and be considerate, in other words, to get along with people" as well as "how to study."

Dorothy Jones is a new teacher, in her first year of teaching, though she is a middle-aged woman with a family. She has just completed all the college work for her permanent teaching certificate, and last year she did six weeks of student teaching under Joan Dexter. Joan is the oldest and the most experienced of the Wright school teachers, being only a few years from retirement. A comparison of their classrooms shows clearly the difference between an experienced production teacher who knows she must discipline the children before she can teach them and the inexperienced production teacher who has not learned classroom control and sees her task solely as imparting the subject matter of the curriculum. This comparison highlights the fundamental nature of production-oriented teaching as an enterprise alien to the genuine interests of most students.

Dorothy Jones's Fifth Grade: Early December. The children are working at their desks and Dorothy is going around the room giving help. The day's work schedule is on the blackboard, with the time to be spent on each subject. The children talk freely among themselves and move about a great deal. They seem to call out questions and comments to the teacher fairly freely. As she gives instructions on the arithmetic lesson they offer critical comments out loud. A child calls out, "Who's that?" pointing to the visitor, who is going toward a chair at the back of the room. When Dorothy replies, several other children call out questions about the visitor. These questions and comments are made in a rather nasty tone of voice, but Dorothy accepts them and answers them.

There is much confusion and noise when Dorothy calls a group of five students to the front of the room to work on arithmetic with her. Even while she tries to conduct her lesson, children call out questions and demands from the room, and Dorothy tries to answer them all or else quiet the questioner. She becomes harassed and at loose ends, going in all directions at once trying to teach the small group, answer questions, quiet talking children, and seat walking children. Children talking or walking about the room generally defy Dorothy's attempts to control them, claiming they are on some legitimate errand such as getting paper or borrowing a book from a neighbor. Dorothy's control of the class seems very tenuous. Children disobey her and talk back to her freely. When she raises her voice to try to control them the room only becomes more noisy and confused as the children shout over her voice. A few students who are trying to do their assignments at their desks are visibly annoyed at the distractions and try to ignore both Dorothy and the other children so they can work. Some even hold their ears as they try to read their texts.

When the time comes for changing subjects, Dorothy says, "All right, put away your books and get ready for science." At this, the room explodes. Most of the children jump up and begin running around the room and shouting. Dorothy can no longer be heard and must outshout all the hollering children. The class is divided into groups for their science projects, and each group has a table with a chemistry set on it. According to Dorothy it is at the request of the children that they are working with chemistry sets. The children seem to be taking effective control of the small work groups, leading them to the tables and starting them working with the chemistry sets, though Dorothy has explicitly ordered them not to start work until she gives permission. The children, or the leaders, interpret her instructions as they please and actually defy her.

Dorothy walks angrily to the back of the room and confronts a girl who seems to be one of the strongest group leaders. Dorothy shouts angrily, "I told you not to begin work." The girl turns and confronts Dorothy directly, and replies in a nasty, mocking voice, "Well, we didn't hear," implying that there was too much noise in the room to hear the teacher's instructions. Dorothy is furious and orders the child to put the jars of chemicals back in the box. The girl puts her hands on her hips, pushes out her chin, and demands with pure defiance, "Why!" At this point the group begins to melt away from behind the leader, putting the chemicals back and wandering away from this painful confrontation. Other children in the room are watching the scene, secretly or openly mocking Dorothy.

This kind of scene occurs day after day throughout the year in Dorothy's room as she attempts to keep the children at their studies without having first achieved dominance by gaining control of the class. She thinks about ways of getting the children to want to learn, such as letting them use chemistry sets for science, but never about ways of establishing her control of the class. In her inexperience she does not know that children must be organized and controlled before they can be taught.

Experienced production teachers like Joan Dexter never make this mistake. They set out to gain control of the class and dominate the children before even beginning to administer the curriculum. They teach the children the classroom routines at the beginning of the year and reinforce them throughout the year so that they are always in control.

Joan Dexter's Sixth Grade: Early in May. Joan has an outline of her "program for the day" on her desk, which she shows the visitor. It has the subjects to be covered that day and times for work on them. When the second bell rings at 8:45 most of the children are in the room and seated at their desks. The rest go to their desks. Joan raps a pencil on her desk for order. When all are quiet she goes and stands at the back of the room and a child comes to the front and reads some verses from the Old Testament, leads the class in the Lord's Prayer, and in the Pledge of Allegiance to the Flag. He then reads from the blackboard the names of the children who are to present things in class, and they come to the front as they are called. Most of them have poems, articles, or excerpts from books to read to the class. When the presentations are finished the child in charge reads the names of those who are scheduled for the next day and goes to his seat. There is some talking from a group of boys who have moved their desks together for the day with Joan's permission, and she warns them as she comes to the front of the room, "You're asking for it." They seem to understand, and they stop talking.

Joan goes to the blackboard and gives a review lesson in rounding numbers. Then she puts some fraction problems on the board for the class to do. A group of girls who haven't mastered rounding gather in the back of the room and Joan conducts a review session with them. The rest of the class works on the fractions. Children occasionally walk about and talk very quietly. They put their papers on Joan's desk when they are finished and return to their desks and sit quietly, reading or just looking around. After a while Joan leaves the group at the back of the room and its members return to their desks. She says, "All right, let me have all the arithmetic now." There are moans and complaints from children who aren't finished. Joan gets angry and says, "I said give me your papers, not start talking." She instructs two children who were talking to write their names on the blackboard at the back of the room. Three sets of upper-grade encyclopedias are wheeled into the room on their carts. Joan tells a few children to get their books. Others complain. Joan scolds them for talking. She sends the rest of the children to the book carts in small groups. The children seem anxious to get the books they have been using but none leave their seats until Joan calls their names. Joan says, "Go to your places and sit down after you have your books." The children sit and get out their social studies projects, for which they are using the encyclopedias. Joan allots time on volumes which are needed by more than one child. Then she says to the class, "When I call your name, you are to come to me and give me a progress report on your research." The children are writing reports on Asian countries for social studies. Joan adds, "In the meantime, if I call your name, write it on the blackboard or give yourself a check, for not keeping busy." A name with two checks after it automatically leads to punishment. All the children are busy at their desks. They seem to be transferring information directly from the encyclopedias to their papers, and even tracing maps from the books. There is little noise or moving about. Once in a while a child comes to Joan with a question from the encyclopedia.

This kind of close, firm control of a class is typical of the experienced upper-grade teachers with a production orientation. They have set definite rules and procedures for classroom behavior and work, and they constantly enforce them, rarely letting an infraction go unreprimanded or unpunished. They organize their classes so they can dominate the children and make them docile learners. They even train the children to administer the curriculum to themselves through their "research work." A result of this latter process was observed earlier in the year when children were presenting reports of their research on European countries.

Joan Dexter's Sixth Grade: Early December. Two girls and a boy are giving their report on Switzerland in the form of a television newscast. They sit behind a table at the back of the room, facing the class. The girl on the left stands and says, "Good afternoon, ladies and gentlemen. Today we have a special program on Switzerland for you." She has all the phony enthusiasm of a real television announcer. She looks at the boy beside her and announces, "First Mr. Franklin will tell us about the products of Switzerland," and sits. The boy rises and recites, "Well, many things come from Switzerland. They have wheat and cows and grass. They make cheese and watches." He continues through his list of unrelated facts, his imitation of a television broadcast faltering in the middle as he rushes through his list. When he is finished he sits and the announcer rises and introduces the other girl, "who will tell us about the geography of Switzerland." This girl also recites a long list of seemingly disconnected facts beginning in a good imitation of a television broadcaster's voice, but losing it as she rushes through her list. When she is finished the announcer gets up again and says she will tell the class "something about the people of Switzerland." She proceeds to recite a confusing series of statements about national origins, languages, and "customs" of the Swiss which cannot possibly make any sense to the children listening. When she is finished, the announcer "signs off" the program and distributes small foil-wrapped wedges of "Swiss" cheese to the members of the class.

The three children here organized a rather entertaining performance in imitation of television, which became an amusing, though unintended, parody of the medium. The lists of "facts" which they had memorized for their speeches did not seem to have much meaning for them, however, being disconnected and without a logical order which might give any sort of coherent picture of Switzerland. These children seem to have performed their research rituals and found their "facts" and presented them in their reports without gaining any knowledge of the country from them. In other words, judging from the illogical and disconnected way they handled their material, it seems that these children had not gained an appreciation of an entity called "Switzerland." Certainly the rest of the children in the class cannot be said to have learned anything about Switzerland from this performance, because the material presented was very disjointed and the presentations themselves were so rapid as to be often incoherent. There is a real possibility here that the children have learned the research and reporting routines required of them by the curriculum and the teacher without gaining any understanding of the subject matter around which these routines are organized. If this is so, then the children and teacher are engaged in an essentially fraudulent enterprise from the perspective of learning, one which is as fake as the "Swiss" cheese distributed by the children at the conclusion of their report.

There are, in contrast, two activities which do engage the genuine interest and enthusiasm of the children in Joan's class. These are recess baseball for the boys and after-school dancing for the girls and a few of the boys. At the beginning of the school year the boys are divided into two baseball teams which are so evenly matched in ability that neither consistently wins or loses. Each day when they can go out for recess the boys race to the ball diamond in the town park adjacent to the school grounds and take up their game with great intensity and enthusiam and, in most cases, total involvement. Joan has to pry them away from the diamond each day at the end of recess to get them back into the room.

The girls have no interest in sports, except in high-school cheerleading, which some of them imitate during recess instead of playing games. They do, however, seem to be anxiously anticipating the social life they will have in junior high school, and all of them stay for the after-school dancing which Joan permits in her room every Wednesday. After dismissal these girls, along with three of the boys, push the desks and chairs to the walls of the room, put on records they have brought from home, and dance for half an hour or forty-five minutes. Since there are only three boys, most of the ten to twelve girls have to dance with each other, but they don't seem to mind this. Joan has considerately provided them with an opportunity to learn a skill which they need and want for next year, social dancing, and no supervision of any kind is needed for this activity. Joan usually spends this time in the teachers' lounge or in another classroom talking with the teachers.

In the upper grades children seem to be able to organize and carry on activities which interest them with little or no help from the teacher. Academic studies, which seem to hold no intrinsic interest for them, must be enforced with a strong classroom organization created and controlled by the teacher. In classrooms without such rigidly imposed structures, such as Dorothy Jones's, the children create something approaching chaos.

Conclusion: An Industrial Model of Education
Production-oriented teachers like Joan Dexter and Wendy Thomas can be successful in their work, both by their own standards and by those of the school system. These teachers, in contrast to those with a craftsman orientation, can make their careers in teaching with only relatively minor adjustments of their educational goals to the organizational structure of the school and the school system. This is because their basic goal is to get the children to master the prescribed curriculum of studies—the fundamental requirement of the educational bureaucracy.

Each production teacher defines her job as imparting at least a minimum uniform education to the children in her class so they will be prepared for their processing at the next stage of school. The experienced production teachers have learned to organize their classroom so they effectively dominate the children and can discipline them to the task of learning the curriculum. In the upper grades they train the children to administer the curriculum to themselves, making the educational process even more efficient. As a result of their efforts a majority of children acquire at least a minimum mastery of the required subject matter, even though they may not come away with any real understanding of the things they have learned.

The end result of a school system organized on the basis of a production orientation would be several types of standardized educational products—if we take into account the "tracking" system of the high school—each type prepared for a different part of the job market or system of further education. Such standardized output implies what might be called an *industrial model* of the educational process. Such a model is in direct opposition to the goals of the other types of educators in the Brookview system, the craftsman teachers and the administrators with the liberal humanitarian and individualistic philosophy of education. It is important, for this reason, to outline the kind of education inherent in the production orientation toward teaching, which is built upon the bureaucratic structure of education in Brookview. This will expose the organizational tendencies of this system (since most successful teachers have or acquire the production orientation), whose consequences will be discussed in the following chapters.

The primary process of industrial production is a series of preplanned operations through which raw materials are transformed into finished products to be used in the economy. This transformation is accomplished in modern industry by workers operating machines under the supervision of foremen. An industry exists and produces because there are markets for its products—a demand or a "need" in society for what it produces. Its products are created for these markets and it stays in business only so long as it successfully meets market demands.

The technical processes by which the raw materials of an industry are transformed into its finished products are designed by engineers, who combine an understanding of the qualities, capacities, and potentials of the raw materials with a knowledge of the processes which can be used to effect their transformation. The techniques they create are embodied in a production plan which in mass-production industries specifies a series of standardized stages through which the raw materials must pass. The operations performed at each stage are scheduled and made into a routine so that they are based on the preceding stage and prepare the materials for the succeeding stage of production. Each piece of raw material or goods-in-process, therefore, undergoes an identical sequence of operations in accordance with a standard technology; that is, all the workers use the same tools in the same manner. Workers in mass-production industries are generally trained to carry out the operations at only one stage of the production process, and these operations are standardized for all workers by the production plan. At the end of each stage there is a quality control check to see that the materials meet the minimum standards for that stage. The finished products are tested to see that they meet the overall standards of the company. Those goods which are acceptable are passed into the market.

Along with the workers who perform the industrial operations on the materials, the supervisors who oversee their work, and the engineers who invent the techniques they use, others in industry specialize in marketing the products and still others manage the entire enterprise, attempting to coordinate all its parts into a profitably functioning whole. Market specialists not only sell the company's products, but also keep the management informed about changes in demands for goods. Managements generally employ specialists to design more efficient production processes and also new products, to meet changing market demands and competition from other companies and products. One important part of an industry's marketing program is creating and disseminating a favorable image of the company, which will help it market all its products. Management also uses image-creating resources to promulgate a favorable image of its own performance in order to maintain its position in the company. Ultimate power in the company rests with the board of directors, which can replace top management if for any reason it becomes dissatisfied with the performance of the company. The board may also bring about the replacement of top management as part of a simple struggle for power over the company.

Viewed in terms of this industrial model, the primary process of education is the curriculum, a series of preplanned stages of learning through which children are put during their twelve years of schooling to prepare them for adult life and particularly for successful entry into the two markets of the public school system—employment and institutions of higher education. The curriculum is divided into yearly stages, and teachers are specially trained to work with children at each of these stages. The teachers are expected to bring about the standardized changes in the children assigned to their grade. They are supervised by administrators and assisted by specialists, who provide materials and advice on ways of getting the children to master various parts of the curriculum. Teachers are trained in colleges in the techniques of teaching the subject matter of various grades. The children, as the raw material or goods-in-process of the educational production system, are tested at the end of each stage to see that they meet minimum standards of learning for that year. At some time during their secondary education the children are "tracked," supposedly on the basis of their abilities and interests, into one of three or four different curriculums which lead into different postschool markets, such as jobs, technical schools, teachers colleges, or universities. At the end of their secondary education the children are examined to see that they meet the minimum standards of the particular track they are on, before being passed into the market.

The entire curriculum plan is developed according to current conceptions of the knowledge and skills people need to participate in different parts of adult life in our society, and the ways in which these can be most effectively learned by children and young people. The subject matter is arranged in the curriculum according to contemporary theories about how and when children can acquire various skills and absorb various kinds of knowledge. These theories are developed by specialists in universities and businesses, who also use their knowledge of the characteristics of children at various ages and the nature of the subjects they are supposed to learn to develop new teaching methods and even whole curriculum plans. Today these new developments in teaching technology are mainly directed at increasing the rate at which children absorb the subject matter, especially in the physical sciences and mathematics. Teachers are taught the new technologies in colleges and in retraining programs conducted by local school systems.

Along with the teachers who impart the prescribed curriculum to the children, the administrators who supervise and advise their work, and specialists who supplement and assist their efforts, school systems maintain specialists who observe the college entrance and job opportunity situation and evaluate the curriculum in terms of changes in market demands. They advise the managers of the school system on skills and knowledge being sought by employers and colleges, and they advise students about programs of study which will maximize their chances for successful entry into various kinds of colleges and occupations. These specialists may also act as public relations representatives of the school system with colleges and other parts of the market, attempting to create and maintain a favorable image of the organization with those who take its products. The managers, or administrators, of the school system attempt to coordinate the activities of its various parts and produce what the public will regard as a good educational product. They also attempt to project a favorable image of themselves and their work in order to secure their positions in the system and gain acceptance of their programs. The board of education has ultimate power over the school system, and if it becomes dissatisfied for any reason with the operation of the schools, it can remove the superintendent either by failing to renew his contract when it expires or by making life unbearable for him so that he is forced to resign.

In summary, I suggest that a bureaucratically organized school system run by teachers with a production orientation would be analogous to a mass-production industry. In the following chapters I shall assess the operation of Wright School and the expectations of parents in relation to this model of education, and examine some of the consequences for the children. In the end I will try to sum up the consequences of the organizational structure of education and the industrial tendencies of the Brookview school system for all the participants.

4 | **Specialists and Administrators**

Introduction

The specialists and administrators who work at Wright School constitute a "second line" of adults involved in the educational process through advising and supervising the classroom teachers. Their work has differing consequences for classroom teachers having craftsman or production orientations, and these different orientations of the teachers in turn affect how the advisers and supervisors carry out their work. The specialists who spend some part of each week at Wright School include six helping teachers, a psychologist, and a nurse. The principal is the sole administrator in a Brookview elementary school, but he is assisted by a full-time administrative secretary. Principal Johnson is also advised by the psychologist, and the nurse regularly pitches in to help on clerical and secretarial tasks. A full-time custodian completes the roster of adults working in Wright Elementary School.

The six helping teachers—so named because they are expected to help the classroom teachers teach their specialties—are specialists in the fields of reading, physical education, music, art, speech, and instrumental music. Aside from the specialists in speech and instrumental music, who teach children outside the regular classroom situation, the helping teachers work mainly in classrooms giving "demonstration lessons" in their fields. The speech "helping teacher" is actually a therapist who conducts three or four small-group sessions in each of her schools for children with speech difficulties or impediments. She rarely has contact with the classroom teachers other than conversations about the progress of the children. The instrumental music teacher is also a 'helping teacher" only in name—for ease of classification in the school system bureaucracy—since he works with a small group of children in each of his schools who are learning to play musical instruments. The remaining helping teachers do work with teachers and children in a regular classroom situation, and we will be concerned here with their work, since it has implications for the different teaching orientations represented in Wright School.

The school psychologist acts primarily as an adviser to the classroom teachers and the principal with regard to discipline and learning problems of individual children. He observes children referred to him, tests them, and discusses their problems with the teacher, and with the parents and the principal where he feels that this will be helpful. Since he is responsible for these services in four elementary schools, he cannot provide therapy for children to any significant extent. When he feels that a child requires therapeutic treatment, he confers with the parents and asks them to secure treatment for the child or to allow him to refer the child to a local clinic. At Wright School, the psychologist also advises the principal about particular children, teachers, and parents and about his educational goals and programs in general.

Principal Johnson is solely responsible for the bureaucratic administration in Wright School, and he has also taken onto himself the task of educational leadership in the school. Johnson came to Wright School when it first opened, seven years before the study, with a strong humanitarian and indiviualistic philosophy of education which he sought to put into practice in the new school. He has instituted many programs over the years and attempted many others, aimed ultimately at developing an instructional program through which some of his goals for education could be realized. The main emphasis of Johnson's principalship has thus been on educational leadership. He tries to organize his work so that bureaucratic administration, or what he refers to as "housekeeping" tasks take as little of his time and energy as possible. He has hired a former career woman as the school secretary and made her, in effect, an administrative assistant by delegating all possible administrative work to her. She does much of the "housekeeping," including keeping all the required records for the school, school system, and state, supervising the allocation of supplies and materials, and running the school communications center in the central office. The Wright School secretary is able to assume these many administrative duties in addition to doing her clerical and stenographic work partly because the nurse, who spends three days a week at Wright School, helps with the office work when she has no nursing to do. She does this of her own accord, out of a desire to be useful, and in the process she learns the administrative routines of the school and is able to fill in for the secretary when she is absent. Johnson has the great advantage of knowing that his routine office work will be adequately handled at all times by one or the other of these women.

As is suggested by the above job descriptions, there is a definite esprit de corps among the members of the "administrative cadre" of Wright School—the principal, the secretary, the psychologist, and the nurse. They form a friendly group socially and are very cooperative in their work. This close-knit administrative work group is partly a result of Johnson's own efforts, in personnel recruitment and in the development of easy social relations among staff members. The group is very important to him, for it provides solid administrative support and professional advice for his performance of the principal's role as he defines it—educational innovation and leadership in the school.

The Specialists

The helping teachers who work with the classes at Wright School have their method of work defined by the school system administration, even though they are teaching different subjects. Officially, these specialists in reading, physical education, music, and art are supposed to be educating the classroom teachers to carry on advanced programs of their own in these areas. As one of the helping teachers said, "We're supposed to be working ourselves out of a job," at least with the more experienced classroom teachers, so that they can concentrate on educating the new teachers who come into the system each year. The Brookview *Handbook for Elementary Teachers* states that because of the small number of special teachers in the system—only twelve all together, two in each specialty, to serve all ten elementary schools—they cannot be used for conducting classroom lessons, but must "concentrate their efforts on giving the regular teachers competence and confidence in these subjects so they can carry out programs on their own, with consultation when needed." Ultimately it was hoped that these specialists would become traveling consultants so that they could reach more of the teachers.

The specialists were only partly successful in achieving their official goal. In general, at least at Wright School, the physical education specialist and the reading specialist seemed to be successful in teaching the classroom teachers new technologies in their areas, which would be games and exercises or reading materials and programs. The specialists in music and art, on the other hand, did not seem to be successful in making the classroom teachers feel competent in these areas. Most Wright classroom teachers would not plan an instructional unit involving extensive use of music or art unless the specialists in these areas were available for teaching their classes. Many of the classroom teachers think of musical and artistic ability as natural talents which they lack and will never be able to learn. The helping teachers try to convince them that even without artistic gifts or extensive training they can carry out a variety of simple music and art programs in their classrooms.

There is a crucial difference between the self-images and the actual work of these two classes of specialists—physical education and reading, on the one hand, and music and art on the other—which accounts for some of the difference in their success in realizing their official goals. This is the difference between technicians and artists. The physical education and reading specialists see themselves essentially as introducing more efficient technologies for teaching the children reading and physical skills. The art and music helping teachers see themselves, although in a modest sense, as artists teaching children new ways of creative self-expression. These quite different self-conceptions and the work-role definitions which follow from them naturally have different implications for their functioning in Wright School.

Elaine Anderson, the reading specialist assigned to Wright School and three other elementary schools, was engaged during the year of the study in introducing a new phonics technique of spelling instruction in some lower grades at the Cedarwood School and the new Science Research Associates reading technology in some upper grades at Wright School. The new spelling technology is known as phonovisual reading, and it is a way of teaching children to identify words by "sounding out" the letters. The following brief observation from a Cedarwood School classroom shows some of the content and method of Elaine's work.

Cedarwood School First-Grade Classroom: January. Elaine enters the room and confers briefly with the classroom teacher. The teacher then goes to the front of the room and conducts a lesson in phonovisual reading, beginning by asking the class, "Shall we show Mrs. Anderson what we learned yesterday?"

Elaine sits in back watching as the teacher puts words on the blackboard and has the children identify the vowel and consonant sounds in them. After this has gone on for a while Elaine comes to the front and takes the class while the teacher goes to the back to watch her lesson. Elaine reviews more sounds and the "sounding out" of words. This is apparently work she taught the class the previous week. She then says that she is going to show the children something new that they can work on this week. She starts teaching the short vowel sounds. After a brief lesson on the short vowels and their sounds, Elaine has the children put their heads down on their desks and confers with the teacher, telling her what seem to be some of the class's weaknesses and suggesting ways of working on them. Elaine then leaves for another first grade to conduct the same sort of lesson.

Here it can be seen that Elaine is teaching the new phonovisual technology to both the teacher and the children, and she is checking each week on how well both have learned their lessons. Elaine and the Cedarwood principal hope to have all the first-grade teachers trained in the phonovisual technology this year so that Elaine can begin with the second-grade teachers next year. One of Elaine's main complaints is that she has so many schools to work in that it takes her inordinately long to get a new program like this introduced throughout a school, even when she has the cooperation and support of the principal and most of the teachers.

Another, more serious problem from Elaine's point of view, is that not all schools will accept all her teaching technologies. At Wright School, for example, spelling is not taught as a separate formal subject until the third grade, though children in the first and second grades are shown the spelling of words they use in writing their stories. The craftsman teachers, with Principal Johnson's support, dominate the education philosophy of the lower grades at Wright School, and they naturally feel that the pure technique, totally devoid of intrinsic meaning, which characterizes programs like phonovisual reading is an anathema to true education. They think that the children are being forced to acquire a meaningless technical virtuosity which may actually harm their chances for a meaningful education. Elaine therefore has no chance whatsoever of introducing these programs into the lower grades at Wright School.

In the upper grades at Wright School, on the other hand, the production-oriented teachers who predominate are very much interested in the latest technologies for teaching reading, and Elaine is busy introducing the SRA program and the SQR (Survey, Question, and Read) method into these classrooms. The SRA program consists of a set of graded, timed reading exercises and tests which are supposed to gradually increase reading speed and comprehension. Elaine introduces the program and its materials into the class of each teacher who requests it, and conducts a demonstration lesson or two. The classroom teacher then assumes the full administration of this technology, with Elaine checking back periodically to see that it is being administered correctly. The SQR method is a technique for reading entire books in such a way as to get their essential points most efficiently. Elaine introduces this method in the upper-grade classes and then also checks back occasionally. The following observations in Wright School upper grades show Elaine going about this part of her work.

Wright School Fifth Grades: January. Elaine walks into Marsha Quinten's fifth grade. The class is out for recess and she goes around the room picking up SRA material which is scattered about. She says that the children will do this picking up once they are well into the SRA program. She then gets out books for the lesson she is going to conduct. When the children come into the room Elaine asks Marsha to have them clear their desks. Marsha instructs the class to do so. Elaine then passes out the pamphlets she has brought. She tells the class, "We are going to do another rate builder. It's been a while since we have done this and you may have forgotten, so listen carefully to the directions." She then reads the directions from the teacher's manual. Elaine reads these very slowly, very distinctly, and very carefully. When she is finished she takes her stopwatch and says, "Ready now . . . go," and the children set to work reading the rate builders. Elaine stops them when the time is up and has them answer the questions on the passage they have just read. She goes through this procedure two more times and then ends the lesson. She organizes the class for collecting and putting away the SRA materials and then goes around to each of them and checks their workbooks to see if they have followed directions and answered questions on the right pages. She has a brief conversation with Marsha giving her advice on conducting the next lesson and then leaves.

Elaine goes down the hall to Joy Neubaum's classroom and walks right up to the front of the room to begin the lesson. She tells the class, "Today we are going to have a follow-up power builder lesson." She then reviews the SQR reading method which they have been taught, asking the children to describe the various aspects of the method. She asks how they "*survey* a book, *question* what is inside, and *read* it." She now explains that they must transfer this skill to the reading they do in their regular lessons. She gives some further instructions and then gives a demonstration power building lesson. After the demonstration she sets the children to work on their power builders, which were distributed before she came. In an apparent explanation of the elaborate directions she has been giving children in these classes, Elaine tells the visitor, "To me the hardest thing to do with children is to get them to follow directions. That's one reason I like the SRA. There are so many directions which the children *must* follow." Once classes begin using the SRA program they are necessarily enmeshed in a complex of rules from which they cannot deviate. Elaine checks the children's work after the power building exercise, has a brief conversation with Joy about their progress, and then leaves the room.

The technological nature of these reading programs and methods is apparent from their names—like "rate builder" and "power builder," which mean increasing speed and comprehension—and from the way they are administered, timed with a stopwatch like work on an assembly line. This is production-oriented teaching in the most extreme form in which it is found at Wright School. All the SRA materials are standardized, not just for the Brookview school system, but nationwide; they are systems developed by a commercial firm and marketed to schools all over the country. The material in them is thus determined by people who have never known these children and their interests, and so it probably has little intrinsic meaning for them. Through them reading is probably transformed from a purposeful activity to an exercise in technical virtuosity like spelling in the lower grades.

Elaine also experiences the typical problem of the production-oriented teacher—control and discipline of the children. She expressed this in her statement about her difficulty in getting children to follow directions. Using materials which have no inherent interest for the children—but rather are assembled on technical bases of graded levels of difficulty—she experiences difficulty in disciplining children to the work. Hence her preference for technologies with elaborate rules which control the children completely once they are disciplined to them and trained in their use. There is no classroom so quiet as one in which all the children are racing as fast as they can through their rate builders or power builders. Such rooms approach complete silence, for the children have been trained and are disciplined to complete concentration on this task.

The mechanical model of the child which is implicit in these spelling and reading technologies that Elaine is helping establish in elementary classrooms is quite explicit in the methods and techniques of the physical education helping teacher, Tom Steinberg. Tom's view of the children is strictly from the perspective of "the machinery of the body," and he sees his purpose as establishing physical education programs which will bring about the most effective functioning of this machinery. At the time of the study Tom was trying to get the President's National Physical Fitness Program adopted in the four schools he served. This physical development program would be analogous to Elaine's SRA reading programs as another nationally standardized teaching technology.

In his actual work with classes, Tom proceeds much as Elaine does in introducing her programs. He has a collection of games and exercises which are supposed to develop various physical capacities of children at different age levels. When he introduces one of these to a class he first describes it very carefully and clearly, then drills the children in it, then lets them run through it a couple of times, then lines them up and has them review all the directions for him. In this way he tries to train classes in games and exercises which will develop the physical skills seen as appropriate for their age. The following observation shows the nature of his work.

Sylvia Baxter's Second Grade: Late September. Sylvia leads the class to one of the outdoor play areas, where Tom is waiting. When they arrive Tom leads the class in a set of exercises which they have apparently already learned. Then he has them make two lines, facing each other about five feet apart. He says, "This morning we are going to work on throwing and catching. Then if you're good we'll have a circle game." He gives elaborate instructions in throwing and catching, demonstrating with a large soft rubber ball. He then gives the ball to the children and has them pass it back and forth between the two lines. He goes up and down the lines correcting the children's throwing and catching. Things get a little out of order as children begin passing the ball back and forth rapidly, playing with it rather than practicing technique. Tom stops them and takes the ball. He makes them stand up straight in their lines. Then he has them repeat the passing and catching directions. Then with a warning not to become disorderly again, he gives them the ball and resumes watching and correcting their throwing and catching technique. After a short time he takes the ball again and has the children form a circle. He gives them the directions for a modified form of dodge ball, which they then proceed to play. When the period is almost over Tom takes the ball again and has the class line up in a single line facing him. He has the children repeat the rules of the game they have learned and then turns them over to Sylvia, who takes them back to their room.

Tom said he likes to work on a regular schedule in the schools he serves in order to build programs of physical instruction over the year. Working occasionally with a class to show them a game or work on a skill is not sufficient to maximize physical development, he feels. Most Wright School teachers are not anxious to have many programs with him, however, simply because he does treat the children in such a mechanical fashion and makes their recess a tedious session of dull lessons rather than a time of enjoyment. As can be seen from the observation, spontaneous play during one of these sessions is actually disruptive and has to be stopped. Tom wants the school to adopt the standards of the National Physical Fitness Program, so that he can get more access to the classes in enforcing these standards. At present the Wright School classes learn and adopt some of the games and exercises he teaches as the classroom teachers want them, and he is consulted for advice on teaching particular game skills which the teachers feel their children need.

The technician specialists represent an impersonal, externally enforced educational process which is mechanically efficient and nationally standardized. This is exactly the tendency identified as a major threat to American education by the educators whose liberal philosophy of education is outlined in chapter 1. The craftsman teachers also oppose this conception of learning as a mechanical procedure encouraging empty technical proficiency. These teachers conceive of real learning as coming from the interests and experiences of the children themselves and, because of this, always intrinsically meaningful to them.

The work of the technician specialists does, however, represent a conception of education basically compatible with the production orientation toward teaching and the bureaucratic organization of education, since it implies that children are raw materials to be put through a standardized shaping process which will produce standard outcomes in the most efficient manner possible. The programs of the technician specialists are spreading through the Brookview elementary schools, and the more they do, the more education here will come to resemble the industrial model.

The helping teachers in music and the graphic and plastic arts have been referred to as artists because they see their work in an entirely different way. They feel that they are providing children with important opportunities for creative self-expression. They feel that this is particularly important because elementary education provides few opportunities for the children to "be themselves" and "learn what they can do" as individuals. They believe that music and art teachers have to work with the children in the classrooms to draw out their creative potential and show them the materials they can use to express themselves. Besides, both of these women like to work with children.

Agnes Morton, the art helping teacher, reported that her goal is not "to make artists" though it does give her pleasure to find "especially creative children" and she tries to make time to work with them. Rather, she said, her goal is to "develop children who are aware of things—who have skill in handling materials and can see the possibilities of materials so that they can always find things to adapt to their expressive needs." She feels strongly that "the arts are a place where people can be themselves," and she wants to "bring out the children and to help them be themselves." Reaching for broader social justification for her work, Agnes said she is "frightened by the idea of so much more leisure becoming available to more people" because "people will not be able to use this leisure," and she wants to provide children with skills and knowledge that they can put to use in their leisure time later in life. Agnes's goals, and her methods for achieving them, are clearly illustrated in the following observation.

Lillian Moore's Second Grade: Early February. Agnes pushes her cart of materials into Lillian's room at 1:00. The class is going to spend the afternoon working on the Eskimo scene they are building in conjunction with their current social studies unit. This scene, a model Eskimo village, stands half completed on a row of tables in front of the windows which stretch across one side of the room. Agnes takes various materials from her cart and shows the children how to make things for their scene, such as cutout cardboard figures with pieces of cloth glued to them to represent Eskimo men, women, and children. These are very simple, clever, interesting devices through which results are obtained very quickly. They seem to give the children a quick sense of accomplishment and to avoid frustration with the work. Lillian has divided the class into "committees" in charge of different parts of the scene, and Agnes starts working with each committee, giving them the materials for their projects and demonstrating how to make the things they need. Soon all the children are industriously at work making mountains, northern lights, Eskimos, seals, dogs, houses, tents, or sleds, or, in some cases, quietly making things of their own which do not seem to be related to the class project. For the remainder of the afternoon, two solid hours, the children remain very busy. Lillian has to discipline only two children who are regular troublemakers. Agnes goes about the room giving advice to the groups on their work. The room has the character of a busy, buzzing little workshop. The materials and techniques Agnes has introduced are so compelling that everyone in the room ends up working on something. Lillian makes Eskimo dolls as Agnes demonstrated, and the visitor models a family of sea lions out of clay, following pictures in one of the children's reference books. At 2:45 Agnes calls on the class to clean up and return the unused materials to her cart. They are reluctant to stop work, and Agnes does most of the picking up. She leaves the cart in the room instead of returning it to the supply room, since the project will be continued the next day.

Agnes is demonstrating the potentialities of materials in this class, showing the children the great variety of things they can make with common materials by using clever techniques. The extent to which she is providing them with an opportunity for creative self-expression is a much more complicated matter. Agnes said that Lillian's was the only second-grade class well enough organized for her to carry out this kind of program. Lillian, she said, organizes her class into small working groups and practices working with them from the beginning of the year, so that by February the groups can spend an entire afternoon working on a project. The project itself is something which has been developed out of the second-grade curriculum, which specifies the Eskimos as one group that can be used for social studies. Lillian is one of the teachers with a production orientation toward education, and the work in her classroom is ultimately based on the prescribed second-grade curriculum. The Eskimo unit is not a project developed out of the children's interests and therefore of vital, intrinsic importance to them. It is a foreign, external subject which has been made interesting to them by especially clever and creative teaching on the part of Agnes; and this kind of teaching is made possible, in turn, by Lillian's highly effective methods of classroom organization and control.

Lillian's Eskimo class project is a highly successful program in the terms of production-oriented teaching. The class has been organized and the children disciplined so that they can work on such a project, and the project, with the help of the art teacher with all her skills and materials and techniques, has been made interesting and involving for the children—and for anyone else who happens to visit the room. All of this, however, does not necessarily add up to an experience of creative self-expression for the children. Teachers with a craftsman orientation would argue that it does not. They would say that no matter how interesting this material has *been made to the children,* it has not *come from them,* and therefore is not a genuine expression of themselves. The lesson represents skillful production teaching technique, but not creative self-expression for children, they would contend.

Hannah Gilbert or Becky Yager, the leading craftsman teachers at Wright School, would never engage in such an elaborate project based on something outside their children's own experience. As we have seen from observations of their classrooms, art projects and other learning whenever possible develop from experiences of the children. They paint murals depicting zoos they have visited or farms they have been to; they make drawings and models of the animals they have seen, and often touched, in such places. Rather than making Eskimos a major project, Becky will use the house being constructed next to the school as the basis of a unit of instruction during the school year. Hannah has her second grade study seasonal changes in plant life on the school campus and in the adjoining school park. For these teachers, in other words, creative self-expression and learning are the same thing. The craftsman equation of creativity and education can be illustrated briefly by one incident in Becky Yager's class.

Becky Yager's First Grade: Early November. There is an amazingly thick fog outside on this day, so dense that you can't see more than a foot or two ahead. All the children walked to school through this "moistury mystery," as one later described it, and the children in the lower grades are excited and awed by the experience. Becky begins a writing lesson in her class by writing on the blackboard "A Fog Story" and asking the children for sentences about the fog. They come fast and furious and many are puzzling. Becky nevertheless puts them on the board, and they make a poem of sorts, expressing the children's experience of this part of their physical world.

> When I walked in it and saw trees it
> looked like pictures it was so foggy
> today.
>
> It feels kind of blurry.
> You can't see too many things.
> Outside it looks gray like a gray fence.
> Sort of a Moistury Mystery.
>
> It's like a cloud lowered down.
> It feels like cotton and the wind
> blows it and you go right through it.
> It feels like a cool breeze that
> doesn't hit hard enough.
>
> It wiggles around a little bit.
> It looks like pictures in the sky.
> It sounds like stars twinkling.

The fog which they have all experienced in an intense way becomes their writing lesson for the day. The fog has been an important experience for the children, and a craftsman teacher makes it part of their learning. Later it will be used, along with other experiences, for lessons in principles of precipitation. Learning and living become merged here into a single, unitary experience for the children. This is the ideal toward which the craftsman teachers strive.

The work of the artist specialists, then, mainly has relevance within the context of the production orientation toward teaching. They try to provide children in this setting with means for self-expression within a context of teacher and curriculum defined activity. This nature of their work can be seen from the following brief illustration of Agnes's work in an upper-grade production classroom.

Marsha Quinten's Fifth Grade: Early February. Agnes wheels a cart full of materials from the supply room to Marsha's classroom. She comes to the center front and says to the children, "We have some interesting things to do that I think you'll like." Marsha has told Agnes she feels she can't go any further in her art program without help, and Agnes has agreed to teach the children crayon and chalk drawing technique. She distributes new boxes of crayons to the children, and tells them they are "going to learn to use them in a new way." She shows a way of holding a crayon, like a wand rather than a pencil, and then shows them how to make a color chart. The children are becoming impatient. They do not as yet have any paper to color on. Agnes asks them to be patient for a minute, and then makes a picture holding the crayon the way she has shown them. She has some children pass out paper, and takes down her demonstration picture. There are groans from the children and Agnes responds by saying she wants them "to do your own pictures" rather than copy hers. She asks them to work abstractly and to experiment with colors. The class is now busy at work with their crayons and paper. Marsha and Agnes move around the room offering advice and help. Marsha shows the visitor two of Agnes's drawings and says, "She did these in half a second. I'm sick." She feels she will never be able to do this kind of artwork and will always have to rely on the helping teachers to teach it to the children. She tells two children to stop working and wait for Agnes to help them. Agnes comes over and gives them some advice with their pictures. Marsha says to the visitor, "See, I know when their work needs something, but I don't know what it needs. You have to have someone like Agnes to show them what they need. I could never do it." The children are so busy with their coloring that only two have to be disciplined during the course of an hour. Toward the end of the lesson Agnes confers with

Marsha, suggesting that they postpone the planned lesson in texture until next week and that Marsha have the children practice with the crayons until then. Most of the children seemed to have enjoyed the lesson. Many of them have done well, according to Agnes. When they see that Agnes is packing up her cart to leave they mob her to show her their work. Marsha sends them back to their seats.

Here, as in Lillian's second grade, Agnes has used her skills with materials and techniques to create an interesting and involving activity. The children seemed to have enjoyed working with crayons and some of them have even picked up the rudiments of the new technique Agnes wanted to teach them. If these children can go on to use this technique to create satisfying pictures of their own, Agnes will have accomplished her goal, providing them with a new means for creative self-expression. These children will then have experienced a creative interlude in their production-organized educational program. There is no doubt that for many children in her schools, Agnes represents just this kind of opportunity. What is unknown is how many continue to want this opportunity as they proceed through their years of schooling. Many in Marsha Quinten's fifth grade simply wanted to copy the picture Agnes had made.

Edith Howard, the music helping teacher who serves Wright among her four elementary schools, works in much the same way as Agnes. She brings various musical instruments into classrooms and teaches the children to play simple tunes on them. She also helps classroom teachers develop musical programs and leads singing assemblies in her various schools. A brief observation will serve to illustrate her work.

Sprucewood School First Grade: February. This class has been working with resonator bells, and the teacher has asked Edith to teach them to play a simple song. As we approach the classroom, Edith says that this is difficult to do with the first grade and can be accomplished only if it is approached correctly. The first thing she does on entering the room is to sit at the piano and lead the children in singing a song they know. Then she gives out the resonator bells (simple xylophones) and shows the children how to play an easy accompaniment to the song. The children play along with Edith, who plays the piano, and all sing. The bells are then given to different children and the lesson repeated, with the children again playing and singing. Edith then brings out some Autoharps and shows the children how to play them. She then tries a combination song with bells and harps. After this experiment she confers briefly with the teacher, suggesting that she have the children practice the Autoharps between then and the next week.

In advanced classes children are using four or five simple instruments in their music exercises. Edith selects these instruments by ease of learning, so that the children can get rapid satisfaction from their use. She sees her work both as teaching basic musical skills to the children and as educating the classroom teachers to the teaching of music. Edith, more than Agnes, sees herself as teaching a subject and less, perhaps, as providing children with a means for creative self-expression. This may reflect the need for the children to learn to play the basic instruments before they can use them as means of self-expression.

The two types of helping teachers, technicians and artists, seem to have relevance mainly for the production orientation toward teaching; reinforcing it, supplementing it, and providing partial relief from its effects on the children. The technicians introduce programs which give greater standardization and mechanical efficiency to subjects prescribed in the curriculum, such as reading and physical education. The artists provide programs to supplement the teaching of various curriculum subjects, such as social studies, in such a way as to engage the children's interest and provide them with the satisfaction of seeing immediate results from their efforts.

The Administration

Hyram Johnson's principalship of the Wilbur Wright School involves two distinct but closely related activities—bureaucratic administration and educational leadership. Johnson himself refers to these two aspects of his job as "paper work" and "people work," giving unhesitating preference for the latter. "Long ago," he explained, "I had to decide whether I was going to work with people or paper. I decided to work with people, so I get the paper work done whenever I find the time." Johnson's highly competent secretary takes responsibility for all the routine paper work. When he has to deal with a major item such as making up the annual school budget to submit to the superintendent, Johnson makes a hermitlike retreat into his office, instructing the secretary to tell outside callers that he is "in conference" and members of the staff that he is doing the budget and doesn't want to see anyone unless it is urgent. In this way Johnson periodically clears his desk of accumulated bureaucratic work so he can carry on his main work of educational leadership, his "people work."

The aim of Johnson's educational leadership at Wright School over the last seven years has been to professionalize, individualize, and rationalize the process of education there. He has been partly successful in each of these areas. He has met with resistance to his programs from teachers, parents, administrators, and the underlying organizational structure itself which in many instances have forced him to settle for less than full realization of his goals, at least for the time being. These areas of professionalism, individualism, and rationalism in the school program are in many respects mutually complementary; but in subtle ways they are contradictory, and so the realization of goals in one area may inhibit the accomplishment of the aims of another area. Johnson's efforts as a whole thus reflect the fundamental conflict in Brookview education between the philosophies and educational goals of the leading educators and the structural demands of the bureaucratic organizations they run.

Hyram Johnson's initial undertaking at the new Wilbur Wright School was to attempt to professionalize the working conditions and the staff itself. Johnson opened Wright School in 1955 with a new set of bureaucratic rules designed to relieve his staff of nonprofessional "police work" involved in minding children when they are not in class. This included eliminating lunchroom duty and before- and after-school duty on the playgrounds. He did this by making a rule at Wright School that children could not bring their lunch to school, but had to eat at home or at the homes of friends, by requesting parents to send their children to school so that they would arrive no more than five minutes before classes began in the morning and afternoon, and by instructing the children themselves not to remain on the school grounds after school. Then he simply did not assign any teachers to playground duty. Parents objected to these rules, and went to the superintendent of schools to get them changed. Children were allowed to stay for lunch in all other Brookview elementary schools, and teachers were supplied to mind them on the playgrounds before and after school. They wanted this at Wright School also. Superintendent Nelson, however, remained true to his policy of decentralized power and responsibility in the school system and stood behind Johnson's actions. Individual principals, he told the complaining parents, had the authority to make these kinds of decisions in their schools and the superintendent could not overrule them.

On the other hand, these rules were extremely popular with the Wright staff, who came to regard this freedom from baby-sitting chores, as they called lunchroom and playground duty, as a major advantage of work at Wright School. They now have two hours a day at school without children: from 8:15 to 8:45 in the morning, from noon to 1:00 in the afternoon, and from 3:00 to 3:30 in the afternoon, when they can grade papers, prepare lessons, or just socialize among themselves. This new opportunity of the teachers for talking together during the school day, mainly during the lunch hour when many of them eat together in the teacher's lounge or kitchen, has very important long-range consequences for the school. It has made possible the development of a definite social structure among the staff. Over the seven years of operation of Wright School, a strong, cohesive faculty group has developed which has a pronounced influence on the work of individual teachers and on the operation of the school as a whole.

The quality of the faculty group which developed at Wright School is partly a result of a second aspect of Johnson's professional development program, finding the best teachers he can. When Wright School opened, Johnson said, he found that he had many teachers who had been sent from other Brookview elementary schools because the principals did not want them. Some of these were poor teachers, he discovered, and over a period of two years or so he performed the difficult act, for him, of not rehiring those who were not yet on tenure, and the very delicate act, for anyone, of convincing those who did have tenure that they would be happier in another school. In recruiting new teachers, Johnson said he looked for normal intelligence, knowledge of elementary-school subject matter, and sympathy for children and an ability to get along with them. The basic requirements for becoming a successful teacher, he feels, are a liking for children and a normal intelligence. He said, "Brilliance alone is not enough to make a good teacher. Knowledge of methods alone is not enough. Teachers basically need enthusiasm for children, character without serious flaws, and normal intelligence." In practice, however, Johnson's hiring policies and procedures are oriented, without his being aware of it, to selecting highly intelligent and earnest people as teachers. Some of them develop into skillful teachers and others do not, but all tend to be bright and to be serious about their work.

It is not surprising, therefore, that the social group the Wright teachers have formed has deep concern for classroom teaching and for education in general. There are many discussions among the teachers, during lunch and before and after school, about problems with individual children in their classrooms and with the subject matter they are expected to teach. In these discussions the teachers share ideas on how to handle particular children and how to teach particular subjects. New teachers at Wright School get most of their initial orientation toward teaching in this way. The teachers as a group also discuss policies of the school and the system which affect their work and develop a consensus through which they actually influence some of these policies. Since principal Johnson takes seriously the delegation of authority and responsibility down through the levels of the school system, he consults the faculty on educational policy for Wright School. Since the faculty members are organized into a cohesive group with a serious concern for teaching and for education in general, they readily take the opportunity to participate in school decision-making. That this participation is real and not merely formal was apparent during the year of the study, when the faculty members, acting as a group, prevented the adoption of two of the principal's policies which they opposed, and brought about the adoption of two programs which they wanted but Johnson disapproved. One of the consequences of developing a dedicated faculty with a strong social unity is that it can effectively oppose the administration.

While engaged in creating a professional setting for work in the Wright School and building a professional staff, Principal Johnson was also inaugurating a series of innovations in the elementary-school program which were aimed at moving toward more individualized instruction. His ultimate goal was to individualize the entire educational process in the school as much as the structure of the organization would permit. He began by introducing the concept of individualized instruction in the classrooms. Children in every classroom, he proposed, should be taught each subject according to their own level of ability rather than the "arbitrary grade-level standards" of the curriculum. The teacher's job is not simply taking a class through the prescribed curriculum of the grade she teaches, but teaching each child as much of a subject as he can master during the year. To help implement this goal, Johnson encouraged the use of "grouping," in which the teacher forms instructional subgroups of children on a similar level of learning in basic subjects, especially in reading. Rather than attempting to teach reading separately to thirty children, or uniformly to the entire class, teachers can instruct four or five groups of children reading on different levels.

The new definition of the teacher's role was at first very upsetting to the faculty. It meant that classroom teachers were responsible not just for teaching the material of their grade level but for teaching on all levels at which children in their class were capable of working. Many teachers resisted this reinterpretation of their role, but, Johnson said, "Some of the teachers were with me and we put it over as the official school program." Johnson also had to sell the idea to the superintendent of schools, he said, in order to get money to buy the books which were needed. Each classroom required textbooks on many grade levels, and implementing the program "was a real scramble," Johnson said, until additional supplies of books could be purchased. "Teachers had to run all over the school borrowing books from other grades" until a wide range of texts could be supplied to each classroom and a central repository of text material created. Even today, Johnson recognizes that "this is a pretty new idea in the school" and, as we have seen, "not all the teachers have picked it up as yet." The result of this policy, if someday it is fully implemented, will be to make Wright School in effect an ungraded elementary school in which all children in all rooms are being taught according to their own level of achievement in the total curriculum.

A close corollary to the idea of individualized instruction as conceived by Johnson is the program of "continuous progress promotion" in which children are kept with their age peers as long as they are at the same stage of social and emotional development, and passed on through the grades regardless of their intellectual accomplishments. Few children are ever left back, or "retained," at Wright School, and when they are it is almost always in kindergarten or first grade, and for reasons of social or psychological immaturity. Remaining with their age peers, so long as they are also their social and psychological peers, is thought to be better for the children than being left back because of learning deficiencies. And, of course, if children are really being taught on their own level in each elementary classroom, it doesn't matter what grade they are in. Pupils at Wright School, then, are to stay in their age-social groups throughout the elementary school years and progress in subject matter at their own rate of learning. This "continuous progress theory" of promotion is coming into practice through-out Brookview, and Johnson is assimilating it readily to his individualized program of instruction at Wright School.

Another part of Johnson's original individualized instruction program was the substitution of individual progress reports for comparative, graded report cards. Johnson felt that the competitive system of evaluating students' progress which is the basis of the traditional report card, with its letter grades in each subject, is incompatible with any program of learning based on the individual capacities and achievements of children. Children should be evaluated, he felt, in terms of their own potential for learning, not in comparison with the performance of other children. Wright School "inherited" the traditional graded report card of the Brookview system when it opened, and Johnson's attempts to institute a noncomparative reporting system met with long and strong opposition from the parents. Anticipating this opposition, he formed a committee of parents and teachers to, as he put it, "look into the whole matter of reporting to parents." The committee examined report cards from hundreds of school systems, Johnson said, and "took what we thought were the best aspects of them all and compiled one of our own." This new form was called a "progress report," and on it children were noted as making "excellent," "satisfactory" or "slow" progress in the basic skill areas: reading, language, arithmetic, spelling, writing, social studies, and science. The parents were advised that "This report indicates the teacher's estimate of the progress your child is making in terms of his own ability. He is not being measured against his classmates or by any so-called norm." They were told that there is bound to be "a wide range of potential ability and achievement" in any group of children of the same age, and that it is the policy of the school "to help each child progress as far as his capacity will allow in all areas of school life." Many parents, however, objected very strongly to the lack of comparative grades on the first "progress report" they received. There was a demand for traditional letter grades which Johnson felt he could not resist, and against which the superintendent felt he could not support him. Parents were therefore given the option of requesting comparative letter grades in the basic skill areas on their children's reports. Johnson then instructed the faculty to actively discourage both parents and children from requesting letter grades.

This individualized instruction and evaluation which Johnson is trying to institutionalize in Wright School is not the same thing as the individually based education which is attempted by the craftsman teachers. Johnson himself recognizes the difference, and says that he favors the *individual education* of the craftsman teachers, but feels that the most he can hope for from the more numerous production teachers is *individualized instruction*, perhaps as a first step in their professional development. Johnson feels that he may be able to convince these teachers to adopt individualized instruction—that is, taking the children through the prescribed curriculum at a pace determined by their own individual abilities, however these are ascertained—but that he cannot at this time train these teachers in the core of the craftsman approach to individual education, which involves the creative act of developing the curriculum around the needs and interests of the children each year.

Furthermore, even though he favors craftsman education philosophically, Johnson fears it bureaucratically. As principal he is responsible ultimately for the children's mastery of the Brookview elementary school curriculum, at least at the minimum acceptable level. In addition, the better the children do in junior high school in comparison with children from other elementary schools, the higher will be his reputation with the administration and the public; so Johnson is under career pressure to have the children at Wright School learn the required curriculum well and is not free to promote all of the educational programs he favors philosophically. He cannot, as he remarked one day, "wait until they are ready for it to teach kids long division. Or map reading. They have to learn these things in the third and fourth grades." Johnson's job as educational leader involves helping the staff find the most effective ways to teach these subjects. I refer to this as his program of rationalizing education at Wright School: discovering and getting adopted the most effective ways of teaching children what they must learn during their years in the elementary school. The unit method of classroom instruction and the Wright school arithmetic program illustrate how Johnson tries to rationalize education in the classroom procedures of individual teachers and the instructional program of the school as a whole.

In the unit method of instruction as devised by modern educators, the teacher picks a complex topic, such as the American Indians, the life of the Eskimos, forests and their uses, or the westward movement (across the continental United States), and builds a long-term program of instruction around it which includes lessons in all the subjects she is responsible for teaching: reading, handwriting, arithmetic, music, art, social studies, and science. Modern educators feel that by involving children in such units they can make the learning of the required curriculum more interesting and involving, and thereby easier and more efficient. The unit is an interest-eliciting device through which educators seek to enlist the children's personal motivations in learning their required subjects.

Principal Johnson tries to teach the unit method of instruction to those teachers who have not learned it when they come to Wright School, and to encourage all teachers to make use of it as a way of promoting efficient curriculum mastery. He described the development of such a program with a teacher at Wright School who "was very rigid and unimaginative in her whole approach to teaching and children." She simply taught the subjects prescribed in the *Curriculum Guide* for her grade, scheduling each day into the same time blocks, as suggested in the *Handbook for Elementary Teachers*, and never thought of relating the different subjects to one another or of trying to relate them to any interests of the children. Johnson wanted her to move toward developing a more unified, flexible form of instruction "in which the children could relate the various skill areas to each other and take an active part in the program." He therefore asked the teacher to take on, as a class project, the planning and planting of the flower beds around the new school building. The project, he said, "was very successful. The teacher and the class developed the whole plan and went ahead and carried it out." This project involved learning in many curriculum areas. Research had to be done on plants, soil, and climate, and this involved reading and science. The flower beds had to be plotted and diagramed, and this involved arithmetic and mapping. Reports of the plans had to be written and circulated among the class, and a final, illustrated report of the project was composed by the class. Johnson felt that the children showed "tremendous enhusiasm" for the project, and that the teacher learned "a new way of teaching elementary school." With this rather simple project, Johnson tried to introduce this teacher to the unit method of instruction.

An example of rationalization of education on the level of the school as a whole is the Wilbur Wright arithmetic program. Johnson sees it as an important part of his job to keep up on developments of new programs and techniques in elementary education, and for a number of years he followed the contemporary research and development in programs for teaching elementary school arithmetic. He feels that arithmetic is the most difficult elementary school subject, because it is taught as a formal system empty of any meaning outside itself. When he found a new arithmetic program which seemed to make mathematics meaningful to children and increase their efficiency in learning it, he brought it to the attention of the Wright faculty with the proposal that they consider adopting it. The program covers the entire six years of elementary school, and to be effective has to be adopted and used by all the teachers in a school. The faculty objected on the grounds that they would lose autonomy in this area of their teaching and that they would have to undergo a certain amount of mathematical reeducation. Johnson argued for the system on the grounds of its efficiency and effectiveness. He brought studies showing that children learned arithmetic more rapidly with this program than with other systems. He pointed out that with this system "children learn the meaning of mathematics" and don't just learn arithmetic "as a series of rote operations."

Under this system, he argued, children would learn *more* arithmetic and would learn *more about* mathematics, and so their education would be significantly improved. He agreed to ask Superintendent Nelson to provide a workshop for the teachers so that they could learn the principles of mathematics they would be expected to teach under this system. Over the course of a year Johnson convinced a majority of the faculty to support this system. Then he announced that it would be put into effect the following year. The teachers who objected had to learn to teach it or leave.

The following year, when the new arithmetic program was introduced throughout the school, parents stormed into Johnson's office demanding to know what kind of nonsense their children were being taught. The new program did not look like arithmetic to them, and they were very much afraid that their children weren't going to learn the arithmetic they were supposed to learn that year. Classroom teachers also faced the indignation of the angry parents, and the school united in the defense of what now became "its" system, against the attack by the outsiders. Parents went to the superintendent of schools to demand that the old arithmetic program be restored at Wright School, but Superintendent Nelson again supported Johnson, saying that it was within the jurisdiction of the schools to adopt programs like this. At the same time, he put Johnson on notice that children from Wright School would be expected to know their arithmetic at least as well as children from other elementary schools when they reached junior high school. Four years later parents at Wright School discovered that more of its students were getting into the new advanced mathematics programs at the junior high school than those from any other elementary school, and opposition to the program, which had been gradually subsiding, disappeared altogether. Johnson was vindicated. The new program did, after all, seem to be more efficient and effective than other arithmetic programs in use in Brookview elementary schools, and the teachers found that they were able to learn to teach it.

The results of Principal Johnson's efforts in educational leadership seem to be the development of more effective production teachers and a more effective educational program, still based on the production orientation toward teaching. How, it may be asked, does he reconcile this result with his educational ideals? "I was rereading John Dewey last night," Johnson remarked one day, "and it's discouraging to see how far we still have to go to achieve even the things he wanted for schools." There is no doubt that Johnson feels the discrepancy between ideal and accomplishment. He also recognizes that it will probably never be resolved so long as he holds to his ideals and does not become satisfied with the reality of his work. The acceptance of his work as an inherently and permanently frustrating enterprise is one of the basic adjustments Johnson has to make to his position. He does what he can to promote the kind of education he believes in, at the same time running the most effective standardized type of education he can. He tries to create a situation in Wright School in which teachers with a craftsman orientation are able to work; but as we have seen, he is not very successful in this, for these teachers seem to leave classroom teaching eventually.[1] On the other hand, Johnson's efforts to promote the most effective form of production-oriented teaching in his school are fairly successful.

This success carries with it a subtle danger for Johnson in the temptation to identify it with the achievement of his real educational goals. So far Johnson seems to have maintained his educational ideals through association with like-minded educators, either through reading their books and passing on their statements of his ideals to the teachers, or talking with those of them who work with him, such as Superintendent Nelson, the school psychologist, and the craftsman teachers. There must be a growing temptation, however, for a man with Johnson's educational ideals to see true creativity, genuine self-expression, and real individual development in the children involved in planting the school flower beds.

1. A year after the study Johnson made Becky Yager, the leading craftsman teacher, general educational adviser for the school, relieved of classroom duties and available to advise all the classroom teachers on all aspects of their programs. Here, then, is a possible opportunity for diffusing more aspects of the craftsman orientation toward teaching to the classroom teachers in Wright School.

Conclusion

The work of the specialists and administrators who advise and supervise the classroom teachers at Wright School seems to have relevance mainly for the production orientation toward teaching. The effect of their efforts is generally to increase the efficiency and effectiveness of production education. In terms of the industrial model of education, they increase the productivity of the educational process, helping it turn out more high-quality standardized products. The craftsman teachers do not find significant support or assistance for their individualized educational program from these other adult workers in the school.

The technician specialists represent a mechanical view of the process of learning. Children are seen implicitly as learning machines to be programmed in the most efficient manner. These specialists acquire and disseminate techniques for increasing the rate of the children's performance or their absorption of the subject matter. Principal Johnson supplements their activities by introducing other technologies, such as the arithmetic program, in all the classrooms. Johnson, however, feels that he is also making this subject more meaningful to the children by introducing a program which teaches the principles of mathematics as well as the manipulation of numbers.

The artist specialists support the work of the production teachers too, by providing materials and techniques to supplement classroom activities organized around the prescribed curriculum. The production teachers look to these specialists to provide them with ways to interest the children in the subject matter through their clever techniques of teaching music and the plastic and graphic arts. The craftsman teachers do not seek the help of the technical or artist specialists, since their conceptions of education and manner of work are foreign to the whole craftsman ideology. For the craftsman teachers, learning is developed out of the interests of the children, and so there is no problem, or ideally would not be, of "interesting" the children in the subjects or devising tricky techniques for getting them to learn the material.

Principal Johnson's work toward the professionalization, individualization, and rationalization of education at Wright School also is relevant mainly in the context of education organized according to the production method of teaching. In particular, taking the children through the curriculum at their own pace and utilizing the most efficient and effective methods of putting across the subject matter given in the curriculum are relevant to the production orientation toward teaching, not to the craftsman orientation. The craftsman teachers in the ideal situation would have a different unit, or curriculum, for each child in their class.

The effect of the work of the specialists and the administrator is, then, to support the production orientation toward teaching. The functioning of these members of the "second line" of adults in the educational system must therefore be seen, along with the bureaucratic structure of the school and the school system, as promoting a more effective industrial type of education. The technician specialists feel basically that this is the best form of education and are pleased to foster it in their work. The artist specialists and the principal, however, oppose this kind of teaching and the industrial type of education. In their work, however, they actually support and improve that which they disapprove.

5

The Parents

Wright School Families

The Wright School neighborhood of suburban Brookview was settled mainly by city dwellers moving out from the Metropolitan City area after World War II. A variety of housing was built here from 1948 to 1965, ranging from moderately priced rental apartments to fairly high-priced homes for purchase. The lowest- and highest-priced housing is the newest in the area, built just before and after the construction of Wright School itself. Until about ten years ago this neighborhood was characterized by two-story, single-family brick homes on small plots of land along winding streets lined with very old trees on both sides of Brookview Avenue. Since then commercial home developers have purchased most of the unoccupied land and have built three kinds of houses on it. Across Brookview Avenue from Wright School they built a colony of twelve two-story red-brick apartment houses, with eight apartments each. These are low-priced housing by Brookview standards. Behind the school, on the other side of the small park which adjoins the school grounds, another developer put up eight blocks of one-story, wood-frame single-family homes on small plots of land. These homes are generally purchased by the families occupying them, though some are rented. The last development to go up in the neighborhood is a colony of large split-level single-family homes built on six blocks which were bulldozed out of the woods on the west side of Wright School, directly adjoining the school property. The well-tended yards of these homes run right up to the school grounds.

As would be expected, a variety of people have moved into the different types of housing in the Wright School neighborhood. Working-class and middle-class—and very upper-middle-class—people live here. There are Jews, Protestants, and Catholics; people of Irish, Italian, East European, German, and English descent; but no "nonwhites," since at the time of the study Brookview was a racially segregated residential community. Those who build and sell homes in Brookview simply would not deal with Blacks. The Wright School neighborhood, is a religiously and ethnically heterogeneous population of working-class and middle-class white people. The working-class families live in the rental apartments across the street from the school and in the small frame homes on the other side of the park behind the school. The middle-class families occupy the older section of two-story single-family homes across Brookview Avenue and the brand-new colony of expensive split-level houses adjoining the school grounds.

A random sample of Wright School families shows that 28 percent are in an upper-middle-class category of husband's income and occupation. This social level consists of two distinct occupational groups—engineers and salesmen. In 1961 these families had an income range of between eight thousand

and twenty-five thousand dollars or more a year, with the younger men just getting started at the bottom end of the range. These families are mainly Protestant and Jewish and live in the newer sections of the Wright School neighborhood, and they occupy the entire colony of split-level houses. The mechanical, electrical, and electronic engineers all have more than a bachelor's degree, and they work for large national corporations or the federal government, many of them on military work. The wives in these families do not work, and on the average have almost a full four-year college education. The engineers constitute 21 percent of the total sample of family heads. The salesman are almost all Jewish and are evenly divided between employees and owners of (mainly small) retail establishments and independent field representatives of large manufacturers of clothing, drugs, and food. They and their wives tend to have some college education, and the wives are not now working.

The second income level of middle-class families in the sample comprises those in which the husbands are fairly high-level bureaucratic managers. They are administrators in large organizations, including a labor union, business, and government, and have incomes of between ten and fifteen thousand dollars a year. They and their wives tend to have almost a full four years of college education, and the wives are not now working. These families constitute 9 percent of the sample of Wright School families. They are Protestant and Jewish.

The three occupational groups so far discussed can be considered solidly "middle-class" in their income, education, occupation, religious affiliation, and "style of life" as judged from their homes. Their life style is exemplified in the new split-level houses in the newest section of the neighborhood. These are large homes having four or five bedrooms, large kitchens with breakfast areas and all modern appliances, dining rooms, living rooms, and "family rooms" where the comfortable furniture and the television tend to be located. In these homes, with the luxury of space to spare, the upper-middle-class families have reintroduced the old parlor, a front room used for display and formal entertaining, whereas their actual "living" goes on in the family room. The living rooms of these new homes of the upper-middle class are furnished like the model rooms on the display floors of expensive department stores, and do indeed serve to display the affluence and taste of the family.

The third income level of Wright School families is made up of those in which the husbands have upper-working-class occupations—technicians, foremen, and skilled workers. In these families half the wives work, and the average family incomes are between eight and fifteen thousand dollars a year. Husbands and wives both have completed high school, but have no further formal education. There are Protestants, Jews, and Catholics in this occupational group, which constitutes 15 percent of Wright School families.

The bottom income level is occupied by families with the husbands in two distinctly different occupational groups, non-technical professional and manual laborer. Families on this level have incomes ranging from six to twelve thousand dollars a year. The nontechnical professionals include people in teaching, the ministry, and accounting, and make up 12 percent of the total sample. All the wives in this group are working. They are all Protestant, and husbands and wives both have at least four years' college education. The laborers, who include machine operators, a truck driver, and other "operatives" make up 15 percent of the family sample. Half the wives of this occupational group are working. Most of the men and women in this group have less than four years' high school education, and a third of the men have only a grammar school education. This group is composed of Jews, Protestants, and Catholics.

These last three occupational groups—the technicians, foremen, and skilled workers, the nontechnical professionals, and the laborers—have similar incomes and similar material components of their life style. Their homes tend to be small, one-story houses with usually two and no more than three bedrooms, or else apartments in the large development, in which there is no room to spare from family living. The furnishings tend to be older, to show the wear and tear of use, and to be entirely for use, not for display. Families in all these occupational categories are carefully saving money now to send their children to college, and in many cases the wives' incomes are earmarked for this purpose. So while not in what is usually thought of as a single class, they share a common low (by Brookview standards) income level and the problems that go with it for people having similar aspirations, such as college educations for their children.

Wright School families as a whole tend to be young, to have many small children, and to be fairly recent arrivals in the suburbs. The average age of the wives is thirty-five, and 90 percent of the families have two or three children. The 410 families sending the 588 children to Wright School have, judging from our sample, over 900 children, of which 25 percent are under elementary school age, 60 percent are in elementary school, and only about 15 percent are of high school age. Of these families 80 percent have come from a city. Fully nine in ten moved to Brookview during the first decade of their married life, and eight in ten have lived here under ten years. Like so many families of their means in the metropolitan area, they have moved to the suburbs to raise their families. The kind of education their children are receiving is one of their most important concerns.

Conceptions of Education

Since education is so important in the minds of parents with children in Wilbur Wright School, it is very easy to get them to talk about their children's schooling, and it is no exaggeration to say that they regard the Brookview schools as the road to their children's futures. Working-class and middle-class parents alike believe that "you can't get anywhere in the world today without an education," and it is very interesting that what "an education" means varies little from class to class. Middle-class families, those in which the husbands are engineers, salesmen, administrators, and even the low-paid nontechnical professionals, all say they plan to send their children to college, while the working-class families, in which husbands are technicians or laborers, say they plan or "hope" to send their children to college. Parents in both classes believe that college, or some post–high-school education at least, is "essential" for boys today. They want their sons to "get somewhere in the world," and for most parents in both classes this means secure, well-paying, and respectable middle-class occupations. Parents in both classes feel that college education would be "a good thing" for their daughters, to give them an occupation, such as teaching, by which they can support themselves, and an opportunity to find husbands who will be good providers. The upper-income middle-class groups are planning to send their daughters to college as a matter of course, and the lower-income middle-class families and the working-class families express the hope that they will be able to help the girls get to college if they want to go.

These parents, then, view elementary school as the beginning of a long process of education by which their children will eventually be prepared for secure middle-class positions in life. They feel that elementary school is particularly important just because it *is* the beginning of the process. Parents from the different social classes and occupational groups conceive of the school's purposes differently and express them in somewhat different ways. But all feel that elementary school is the place where children should acquire the basic academic learning, a positive attitude toward education, and efficient study skills which will help carry them through the long years of schooling ahead. Each division of school—lower elementary, upper elementary, junior high, and high school—is seen as preparatory for the next, teaching the children the things they will need to know to get along well. As education itself is seen as a means toward economic security and social status, so each stage of the process is seen as a means to success in the next.

Working-class parents conceive of the "basic academics" fairly narrowly as "the three Rs" of reading, writing, and arithmetic. In the lower grades they feel that most school time should be spent gaining a grounding in these subjects, especially reading; and in the upper grades they feel that the children should be taught these subjects in such a way as to "be prepared for junior high school."

These working-class parents are very concerned that their children become accommodated to school and learn its ways.

They feel that their children must learn to like school in these earliest elementary years. As one mother said, "In the school you have to make the children interested in learning and willing to work, so they can get ahead." Especially in the early grades they feel that it is necessary to "instill a desire for learning," and "give them the feeling learning is very important" so that their children will want to continue beyond the legally required years of schooling—which means beyond what these parents achieved. These parents don't want their children to leave school as soon as the law allows, as most of them did, but to continue on to receive some form of education beyond high school. They expect the elementary school to help socialize their children to the educational process so that they will stay in school and be successful. One mother, for example, said, "Kindergarten affects all their later attitudes in school. You need the kind of person you can feel affection for so they'll like her," and through their liking for the kind teacher, come to like school. Some of these parents feel that the school staff should somehow "*teach* them to like school" in the same way that they teach some subject, such as arithmetic. Others, however, see this as more of a process of "making school interesting and enjoyable" so the children will come to like it and want to do the work required. In both cases, creating a positive attitude toward school is seen as instrumental; children must be socialized to this organization and its activities so that they will attain success in it. Success, of course, is judged by the children's grades and their evident mastery of the basic academic subjects.

The other important aspect of becoming accommodated to the school and its ways is learning effective methods of study. These working-class parents have a number of ideas of what makes for "good study habits," as they refer to them. Mainly, they feel that the children need to be disciplined in the classroom—to be taught obedience and respect for the teacher so that they will be willing to do the work assigned them. One mother goes so far as to say that the children need "to have a little fear of the teacher as a person who makes them work." Another feels that teachers should "reinforce home teachings of respect and manners," in the demands they make on the children in school. These parents see good study habits mainly as diligent application to the assigned school work by children controlled through fear of the teacher or respect for her authority. An external set of materials, the subject matter, is learned through the application of an external control, the power and authority of the teacher, reinforced by that of the home.

Middle-class parents also believe that the primary task of the elementary school is teaching the basic academic materials to the children. However, they define "basic" more broadly than working-class parents do. The middle-class parents are willing to include science and social studies along with reading, writing, and arithmetic as basic elementary-school subjects. A few, among the nontechnical professionals in particular, go so far as to say that art and music are also basic elementary-school subjects. One mother, for example, said that children should not only "learn to read and write and count," but should also "get to know about the geography and history of different countries of the world." Another said that the elementary school curriculum "should include history, social studies, art, and music [because] it's important for children to learn a love for these." The "three Rs" plus history, geography, and science were seen by most middle-class parents as the basis of an elementary-school education. They were emphatic, also, in stating that the children should be taught as much of the basics as they could absorb in elementary school. A frequently expressed sentiment among middle-class mothers was that the school "should teach them the most they can possibly learn" of the subject matter. This desire for educational efficiency is similar in effect to the working-class parents' desire that the school prepare the children for junior high, in terms of subjects taught and of work habits developed. Middle-class parents are very much concerned that their children be as well prepared for junior high as children in other classes in Wright School and in other Brookview elementary schools. They want their children to get a background which will put them in a favorable competitive position for the next stage of the educational process. The middle-class parents conceive of the educational process not only in terms of a series of stages, each of which prepares the children for the next, but as one in which each stage is also seriously competitive. And they want their children to do well in this competition.

Middle-class parents feel that learning has to be made attractive to the children so they will want to do well at each stage and to continue with their schooling through college. They say that the school should "get the children interested in learning," and "hold their interest by the way it presents the material." One mother said this could be done by recruiting teachers "who are excited and interested in their work and who stimulate the children to learn." The more sophisticated level of these mothers' conceptions of the development of positive attitudes toward learning is illustrated by one who said the school must "get the child attuned to school emotionally and psychologically so he'll want to do his work and continue his education." These parents see the approach which the school staff takes to the children as crucial in developing positive attitudes toward learning. They look for teachers who are "enthusiastic" about the work and convey this feeling to the children, inspiring the children to want to work hard—to be their own taskmasters, so to speak. Here, as in the conceptions of basic subject matter, the parents in the nontechnical professions had perhaps the broadest conception of a positive attitude. One spoke of school experience as "giving the children a good feeling for school, showing them that learning can be fun, so that they'll want to continue in their work and do better because they like it." Others extended this to the idea of a "love of learning" which they wanted the school to instill in their children. These parents saw a love of learning as instrumental in bringing about greater efforts at achievement, but here we also meet for the first time a conception of learning as something to be valued for itself. These professionals, some of whom are employed in education themselves, want their children to value learning as something good and pleasurable in itself, and not only a means to a career and material success. For the most part, however, middle-class parents, as we have seen with working-class parents, want their children to like school so they will be motivated to do the work and get ahead in the system.

Middle-class parents, finally, see the elementary school as the place where their children acquire the basic study skills which will contribute so much to their success in the educational system. These parents feel that they can teach these skills to some extent at home, provided the school assigns homework which they can supervise. A few parents in this class also think the schools should help the children think as individuals, as a tool for learning. As one mother said, "The school should provide an encouragement for learning; pique their curiosity about something and then show them how to satisfy it by using the resources available." The middle-class parents, like those from the working class, want the schools to teach efficient learning skills, but they also conceive of independent inquiry as one of these skills, along with more routine types of "good study habits."

It should be noted that not all parents have this basically controlling attitude toward their children or this instrumental attitude toward education. A few parents, in both the working class and the middle class, did say they want their children to be "whatever they want to be" or "whatever they turn out to be," and to go on to college "if they want to, and if they have the aptitude." These parents tend to look on the school less as a long graded processing leading to a standardized product and more as an experience which can be valuable for the children in itself if handled well by sensitive people. This small minority of parents believes the schools should provide the children with "opportunities for self-expression" and with a chance "to discover themselves" rather than systematically socializing them to a standardized curriculum. One working-class mother speaking of her daughter said, "I wouldn't want to push her into anything she wasn't interested in." If the girl wanted to go to college this would be all right "if she wants, but I won't push if she isn't interested." This mother wanted teachers who "understand children and take a real interest in them." She felt that the "happy and pleasant teachers who are genuinely interested in the children," which her daughter has are far better than the teachers she had, "who were old women who just gave work and didn't care really about children." This working-class mother appreciates the fact that school is a pleasant place for her child where there are people who take an interest in her as a person.

The middle-class version of the more casual attitude toward child-rearing and education was expressed by the mother who said she wanted her boy to go to college and then "be what he wants." She went on to explain that although she and her husband felt it was their "duty to instill in him a desire for college" they did not feel they should "push him into anything occupationally" but rather should let him find what he wanted to do for himself. She felt that one of the most important things elementary school could do, along with giving a good grounding in the academic subjects, was to teach children to think independently. She was happy with her child's teacher this year because "she is teaching them to think as individuals, and this is what they need as much as anything else" they can get from school. This is consistent with her desire that her boy go to college but be able to choose his own life for himself from there on. These parents want their children to be able to make choices and think independently, within an acceptable social and educational context.

Evaluations of Wright School
It is to be expected that parents of children at the Wilbur Wright School will evaluate the school program and staff in terms of their conceptions of education. They will judge the performance of the school, in other words, in terms of their expectations of what its program will mean for the plans they have for their children. The information by which parents evaluate the school's work comes from a number of sources: mainly reports their children bring home and the work they see their children doing, but also from conversations with other parents, conversations with the school staff, and information sent home by the Parent-Teacher Association. On the whole, the parents have very little firsthand contact with the school. Only 30 percent of the mothers reported that they visited the

school more than four times in the course of a year. This means that they evaluate school programs mainly by what the children tell them and show them they are doing and what they hear from other mothers, who have also gotten most of their information from the children. On the basis of this knowledge, the majority of parents seem to feel that the children are not being worked hard enough and therefore are not learning as much as they could be. They feel there is too much "playing" in the school, too much attention to "social adjustment," and insufficient demands for achievement. A minority of parents, on the other hand, are satisfied with the results they see in their children and feel the school is doing a good job in educating them.

Criticism tends to be on a kind of production-efficiency basis. Some parents feel that too much of the school day is spent on activities other than learning the academic "basics"—whether they give this a narrow or broad definition—and that the school does not demand enough learning from the children—doesn't "push" them hard enough in the "academics," as some of the mothers put it. They are very critical of the idea of taking the children through the curriculum "at their own pace" because, as one said, "they'll slack off if you don't push them to work." These parents feel that the children need to be given more work, and the teachers need to "see that they do it." Such parents feel that their children are capable of learning more than they are being taught. They feel that "grouping" in classes is inefficient because "there's too much time when they aren't working with the teacher and have nothing to do" in the classroom. They would prefer homogeneous classrooms in which all children would be taught the same material at the same time, and the entire time would be spent on teacher-led instruction. Some of these parents feel that the children "are tripped to death," as one put it, though, she added, "it's probably fun for them." She failed to see going on trips as having anything to do with learning, but considered it as a pleasant diversion from schoolwork. The unit method of instruction is completely foreign to these parents, and when they see classes making Indian arts and crafts, or planning and planting flower beds, or watching a house being built, they assume that these are digressions rather than parts of the learning process. These critical parents, looking at the unfamiliar procedures of both the craftsman and the production teachers at Wright School, fear that their children are not going to get a sufficient education in the academic fundamentals.

The critical parents are very much bothered because teachers at Wright School are allowed to teach the curriculum in their own ways in their classrooms. This means that children in different sixth grades, for example, may be studying different things at a particular time. Parents become afraid that their child's class will not cover all the material that is covered in another class, and that their children will not learn as much as those in other classes and therefore will be at a disadvantage the next year. They want the principal to enforce a uniform way of teaching the curriculum so they can be sure their children learn "all they are supposed to know" in each grade.

Along with more work and uniform teaching, these parents would like to see stricter discipline in the school. They feel that the children are given too much "freedom" at school and are not "kept in line" the way they should be. From reports of their children, these parents have concluded that the children exercise effective power in some of the classrooms at Wright School. This, they feel, is scandalous and is further evidence of the principal's lax supervision of his staff. Some feel it undermines parental authority in the home. Children, these parents feel, should be made to "show obedience and respect for adults," by which they seem to mean they should be under their direct control at all times. These parents want greater efficiency in teaching, more standardization, and tighter control in the classrooms.

Parents who have an overall favorable evaluation of Wright School feel, first of all, that the school "covers the basic studies well," as one mother put it. These parents see that their children are "happy and seem to be learning," and so they are satisfied with the school. Some of them see as an advantage the very variety and freedom which other parents condemn. They feel that "there are more creative opportunities and more encouragements of creativity here" than in other Brookview elementary schools. These few parents feel that it is a very good thing that "they encourage self-expression" and feel this gives Wright an advantage over the other schools. Parents with a favorable attitude toward the school also claim that Wright School graduates do well in junior high school.

Conclusions: Consequences for Education

If the majority of parents exercised effective influence on Wright School, they would move education there in the direction of a more standardized industrial production model. They would have their children be taught more, taught the curriculum in the same way as all other children, and be kept under direct control of the teacher during their school hours. They would make it impossible to implement either an attenuated version of craftsman teaching or the advanced version of production teaching being introduced by Principal Johnson. The critical parents oppose all the programs which Johnson and the Wright teachers feel are the most effective new methods of education. Children on a trip to a dairy farm, working on an Eskimo unit, or sitting at their desks doing something while the teacher works with a reading group are not *working* in the eyes of these parents, and therefore are not *learning*. This, in their opinion, is a waste of school time and a demonstration of the inefficiency of education at Wright School.

The majority of parents, however, have very few direct contacts with the school, and make no attempt to change the practices there. Some feel that even though they may disapprove of practices in the school it would be presumptuous of them to criticize the specialists and demand that they adopt some other program. Other parents feel that attempting to influence the educators brings no results, even though it should be done. These are the people who, when they are very upset by a school program such as the new arithmetic, may go in a group to the principal to complain, and when this is of no avail, may go to the superintendent of schools. The influence of the majority of parents on educational practices at Wright School is exercised in this indirect way, by the threat that they may initiate a group protest if they are strongly opposed to a school program. The possibility of such a protest is in the mind of the classroom teacher when she contemplates a radical new program in her class (and this would apply mainly to craftsman teachers) and in the mind of the principal when he contemplates a radical new program for the school as a whole.

A small number of parents, however, do become continuously active in the affairs of the school. These are the women who organize and manage the Parent-Teacher Association. At Wright School, the long-time leaders of the PTA are women who were originally motivated to become active in school affairs because they opposed the policies of the new principal. They came to work in the school to "see what was going on there," as one said, and to see what they could do "to make sure our children got a good education." They were genuinely afraid that this new principal, with what seemed to them to be "wild ideas about education," and some of the teachers were going to deprive their children of a good education. These women had to recruit other mothers to help carry on the work —there are six officers and twenty committee chairmen in the PTA organizational structure—and many of these women were motivated by a desire to help the school, and so help their children, without feeling in any way critical of the principal or the teachers. The PTA then became staffed with women very much concerned with good education for their children—some who were afraid the school would not provide it, and others who assumed it would.

Principal Johnson worked closely with the PTA from the very beginning. He said he had learned from the principal he had worked under that "you have to be the controlling influence in the PTA" and that the principal, if he was active in what is really a parents' association "can be the most influential person in the group." It is through his activity in the association that the principal moves it to support his policies, Johnson said. By working closely with the PTA women from the beginning, Johnson has succeeded in turning the organization into one which supports the school and his administration and, as part of the larger Brookview PTA Council, actively supports the liberal candidates for school board office and stands behind the administration of Superintendent Nelson. He has done this by working hard to convince them that they all have the same interest—"the very best education for the children"—and that this interest is best realized in the kind of educational program he and Superintendent Nelson stand for. Over the years Johnson has successfully turned their desire to support good education into support for the kind of education he, and the superintendent of schools, define as good education. The women who are active in the school, then, whether they originally held positive or negative views of educational practices there, now tend to support the school, Principal Johnson, and the teachers. They have to a large extent been co-opted into the system some of them began by opposing.

Through his effective influence in the PTA, Johnson is now able to use the organization to protect the school from criticisms which are periodically brought against it by groups of parents. He must at the same time, of course, maintain the support of the women who run this organization, which means maintaining smooth relations with them and between them and the school faculty. This occasionally puts him in a difficult position, such as putting pressure on the faculty to join the PTA and attend its functions even though it was basically a parents' group.

In conclusion, it can be seen from this study of the parents' attitudes toward education that behind the school and its different kinds of programs there is a large body of opinion which is hostile and opposes the programs. The kind of education attempted by the craftsman teachers is understood and supported by no more than 1 or 2 percent of Wright School parents, and Principal Johnson's own kind of enlightened production education receives only minority support from the parents. The great weight of parent opinion is clearly behind a program which more closely approximates the industrial model of the educational process. They want the schools to use more standardized processes to produce more educated children more efficiently.

6

Children's Response to Educational Organization

Organizing the Classroom

The standard curriculum of the Brookview school system and the production type of teaching in Wright School taken together create, I have suggested, a situation in education which is analogous to mass production in industry. The industrial model of education is of course an analogy, however, and not an identity. The basic difference between the industrial and the educational systems, which accounts for some of the important characteristics of the organization of education at Wright School, is the fact that the raw materials of the educational system are human beings. The children, willful creatures with needs and desires of their own, as well as modes of expressing them which are some-what developed before they enter school, cannot be expected to take their processing through an industrial system in a passive manner. The school must find ways to make them willing to submit themselves to learning what is expected of them. Basically, the children have to be organized into closely controlled formal classroom groups before they can be expected to learn the prescribed curriculum.

Experienced educators like Principal Johnson feel that it is necessary to organize classrooms very carefully before the children can be taught the required subject matter. Johnson sees classroom organization of a rather formal type as being the only way teachers can effectively control children and discipline them to the curriculum. He advises teachers to concentrate on organizing their classrooms as smoothly functioning groups during the first part of the year, and he tries to advise new teachers on how to create and maintain strong classroom organization. At the beginning of each year Johnson gives the teachers a written guide containing suggestions about this, which reads in part as follows:

1. Discipline: Train children for self-discipline rather than relying on policing the room to keep order.

2. Mechanical Routines: Get them established early, to your satisfaction, and don't settle for less—how to pass papers, exchange papers for correcting, stand quietly as a group, leave the room as a group, move through the halls as an individual or in a group, etc.

3. Establish Your Authority: Greet the class with a friendly smile but be firm in following the outline above. Permit no attempts at dictation by the aggressive child. Spend no time in idle conversations and the "What did you do last summer?" sort of thing.

4. Organize Your Class Immediately: The efficient functioning of any group of people requires guidance. Children need and enjoy the security that stems from a well-organized daily routine. They will lean strongly on your adult leadership.

5. Be Friendly: Gradually work toward a close personal bond with each child. Even the trouble-maker should feel that you like him although you do not approve his actions. Probably the most important single factor which determines how a child learns is his relationship with you.

We have seen that competent teachers with both the craftsman and the production orientation learn early in their careers to organize their classrooms along rather formal lines as a means of controlling their classes so they can teach the children. They spend the first part of every school year creating little bureaucracies in their classrooms, with formal rules, rigid routines and schedules, and strict authority, before they attempt to begin systematically teaching the curriculum. Through this bureaucratic organization, which they carefully maintain throughout the year, the successful teachers dominate and control the children and gain the compliance of most of them with their educational processing.

Teachers with different orientations, of course, respond differently to the necessity of creating formal classroom organizations. The craftsman teachers feel that it prevents them from establishing genuine personal relations with the children. In a bureaucratic organization all participants are playing limited roles, and their relations are between people playing specialized roles, not between whole individuals. These teachers become doubly alienated from their work when they must teach the required school system curriculum, which they do not want to do, and when to do this they must create a formal classroom structure which isolates them from personal relations with their pupils.

Some production teachers, such as Wendy Thomas, may lament the loss of spontaneity which this bureaucratic role-playing causes, but it also facilitates the production teachers' work. The pupil role as learner of the prescribed curriculum exactly complements their definition of their role as administrator of this curriculum. The teacher-pupil roles so defined are congruent with the structure of the school and are enforced by the work of the specialists and administrators and supported by the majority of the parents.

In this chapter we shall examine the way in which classroom organization controls pupil behavior and teaches the pupil role, and the different meanings this role may come to have for the children.

Basic Training for the Pupil Role in Kindergarten

Kindergarten is the place in which children begin to learn the pupil role. At the core of this learning is a set of classroom routines which the teacher introduces and then trains the children to follow. Kindergarten teacher Diane Ross said she hated the first month of school because "in September, everything has to be done rigidly, and repeatedly, until they know exactly what they're supposed to do during the day." "However, by January," she went on, "they know exactly what to do and I don't have to be after them all the time." This training takes a long time in kindergarten, and it is done by *drilling* the class in the daily routines. Kindergarten, then, is the "academic boot camp" in which children become conditioned to their first bureaucratic role.

Kindergarten classroom routines are introduced gradually during the first few months of the year, and the children are drilled in them until they give regular compliance. By the end of the school year, the successful kindergarten teacher has an effectively organized classroom in which the children follow her routines automatically, having learned all the command signals and the expected responses. Edith Kerr's kindergarten shows this tight bureaucratic structure and functioning near the end of the school year.

Edith Kerr's Kindergarten: Last Week in May. The two Wright School kindergartens are at the end of the primary wing of the school, jutting out from it at angles so that they have windows running down two sides. They are very light, brightly colored and decorated, and filled with children's toys, games, picture books, and so on, all making a very pleasant environment which would seem to be attractive to children. Edith's room is divided into a number of different activity areas. Two easels and a paint table near the door create a kind of passageway into the room. A wedge-shaped space just inside the front door has been made into a teacher's area by placing her things there: desk, file cabinet, piano. Past this area, to the left, is the book corner, marked off from the rest of the room by a puppet

stage and a movable chalkboard. In it are a display rack of picture books, a record player, and a stack of children's records.
To the right of the entrance, beyond the easels, are the sink
and clean-up area. About halfway down the length of the room,
four large round tables with six chairs at each are placed near
the walls, two on each side, leaving a large open area in the
center for group games, block building, and toy truck driving.
Windows stretch the length of both walls, starting about three
feet from the floor and extending almost to the ceiling. On the
shelves under the windows are kept all the toys, games, blocks,
paper, paints, and other equipment of the kindergarten. In the
rear corner on the left is a play store with shelves, counter,
merchandise, and cash register; in the right rear corner is a
play kitchen with stove, sink, ironing board, and a bassinet with
baby dolls in it. A sandbox standing against the back wall separates these two areas. The room seems light and bright and filled
with things children would like.

At 12:25 Edith opens the outside door to the primary wing
and admits the children waiting there for the afternoon session.
They hang their sweaters on hooks outside the classroom door
as they come in, and then enter the room and arrange themselves in a semicircle facing the chair Edith has placed in the
center of the floor. Edith follows them in and sits in her chair
checking attendance while waiting for the bell to ring. When
she is finished she asks the children the date, the day, and the
month of the year. Then she asks how many are in the class,
how many are present, and how many are absent.

The bell rings at 12:30 and Edith puts away her attendance
book. She introduces the visitor, who is sitting against the right
wall taking notes, as someone who wants to learn about schools
and children. She then goes to the back of the room and takes
down a large chart labeled "helping hands." Bringing it to the
center of the room, she tells the children it is time to change
jobs. Each child has some task, signified by his name on a paper
"hand" placed next to a picture such as a broom, a sponge, a
blackboard, a milk bottle, a flag, a Bible. Edith asks the children who wants each job, and rearranges their "hands" accord-

ingly. Returning to her chair, Edith announces, "One person should tell us what happened to Mark." A girl raises her hand, and when called on says, "Mark fell and hit his head and had to go to the hospital." Edith adds that Mark's mother had written saying he was in the hospital.

Here we might pause to note how Edith has structured the class so far. The children have literally known their place from the beginning. When they came in and saw her chair in the center of the room, they arranged themselves around it without a word from her. Edith then took them through a very rigid locating procedure in which they are asked to find themselves in adult terms of time and place—they are asked to give the date, the number of children present, and then to decide what new job they want. She has, of course, completely structured the room physically, having divided it all into special activity areas, with the exception of the open space in the center of the room. Anticipating a potential source of disruption of her control she has someone give a formal statement of the unusual event that has occurred, a class member's being sent to the hospital. She has also introduced the visitor and defined his purpose, thus structuring this other unusual event into the class organization. Of course during this time the children have been interacting among themselves, but in a very subdued way. They have whispered to their neighbors, poked one another, made whispered general comments to the group, waved to friends on the other side of the circle. None of this has been disruptive, and Edith has ignored it for the most part. The children seem to know just how much interaction of each kind is permitted: they may greet in a soft voice someone who sits next to them, for example, but may not shout greetings across the circle to a friend, so they wave instead. With the exception of one large and noisy girl, they all seem to know the limits of unstructured interaction and to stay well within them. Whenever this interaction might threaten classroom order, Edith resumes control by reimposing her structure, as will now be seen.

At 12:35 two children arrive. Edith asks them why they are late, then sends them to join the circle of children on the floor.

The other children vie with one another to tell the newcomers what happened to Mark. As they become disorderly Edith asks, "Who has serious time?" The class becomes quiet and a girl raises her hand. Edith nods to her and she gets a Bible and hands it to Edith, who reads the Twenty-third Psalm while the children sit quietly. Edith helps the child in charge begin the Lord's Prayer, and the class follows along for the first set of sounds, then trails off as Edith finishes by herself. They all stand and face the American flag hanging next to the door, and Edith leads in the Pledge of Allegiance to the Flag, with the children again following the familiar sounds as far as they can and Edith finishing up alone. Edith asks the girl in charge what song she wants and the child replies, "My Country." Edith goes to the piano and plays "America," singing it as the children try to follow her words.

The teacher, in this interchange, uses her classroom structure to break off interaction which is becoming a noisy situation that she does not control. "Serious time" is the first of six "times" into which Edith has her classroom day divided. The children by now have learned what is expected of them in each of these periods, and they obediently assume the appropriate behavior and attitude when Edith announces the beginning of one of these "times." The day has been programmed for them, and the children have been trained to go docilely through each of its parts. Sharing time, which follows, provides some particularly informative examples of the contrast between this teacher-structured world and the children's own world of experience.

Edith returns to her chair at the center of the room and the children sit again in the semicircle on the floor. It is 12:40 when she tells the children, "Let's have boys' sharing time first." She calls the name of the first boy sitting on the end of the circle, and he comes up to her with a toy helicopter. He turns and holds it up for the class to see. He says, "It's a helicopter." Edith asks him, "What is it used for?" and he replies, "For the army. Carry men. For the war." Other children join in suggesting, "For shooting submarines," "To bring back men from space when they are in the ocean." Edith sends the boy back to the circle and asks the next boy if he has something. He says no, and she passes on to the next. He brings a bird's nest to her. He holds it up for the class to see, and Edith asks, "What kind of bird made the nest?" The boy replies, "My friend says a rain bird made it." Edith asks what the nest is made of, and various children reply, "mud," "leaves," "sticks." There is a bit of moss woven into the nest and Edith tries to describe it to the children. But they are more interested in seeing if anything is inside it, and Edith lets the boy carry it around the circle, showing children the insides. Edith tells about some baby robins in a nest in her yard, and some children tell of baby birds they have seen. Some children ask about a small blue object in the nest which they say looks like an egg, but Edith calls on the next boy to bring what he has. A number of children say, "I know what Michael has, but I'm not telling." Michael brings a book to Edith and then goes back to his place in the circle. Edith reads the last page to the class. Some children tell about books they have at home. Edith calls the next boy and three children say, "I know what David has." "He always has the same thing." "It's a bang-bang." David goes to one of the tables and gets a box, which he brings to Edith. He opens it and shows her a scale model of an old-fashioned dueling pistol. When David does not show it to the class, Edith tells him to turn around and show it to the children. One child says, "Mr. Johnson said no guns." Edith says, "Yes, how many of you know that you aren't supposed to bring guns to school?" Most of the children in the circle raise their hands. She calls on the next boy, who brings two toy soldiers to her which the children enthusiastically identify as being from "Babes in Toyland." They want these passed around, but Edith calls on the next boy, who brings an American flag. She asks him what the stars and stripes stand for, and admonishes him to treat it carefully. She asks him, "Why should you treat it carefully?" He replys, "Because it's our flag." She congratulates him, saying, "That's right."

Show and tell has lasted twenty minutes now, and during the last ten one girl in particular has announced that she knew what each child called upon had to show. Edith has asked her to be quiet, but she has continued to speak "out of turn." Four children from other rooms have come in to bring something or borrow something from Edith. Those with requests are asked to return later if the item isn't readily available.

Edith now asks if any of the children told their mothers about their trip to the zoo the previous day. Many children raise their hands. As Edith calls on them, they tell what they liked at the zoo. Some children cannot wait to be called on, and shout out things to the teacher, who asks them to be quiet. One child says, "I liked the spooky house," and the others chime in enthusiastically, some pantomiming fear and horror. Edith is puzzled and asks what this was. When half the class tries to tell her at once she raises her hand for quiet and then calls on individual children. One says, "The house with nobody in it"; another, "The dark little house." Edith asks where it was in the zoo but the children cannot describe its location in a way which she can understand. Edith makes some jokes but they involve adult abstractions which the children cannot understand. The class has become quite noisy now with children speaking out to make both relevant and irrelevant comments, and three little girls have become particularly assertive.

The child level of perception, which Edith has constantly ignored during this period has finally erupted into the classroom with the children's recollection of the "spooky house," and Edith temporarily loses her control of the class. She has consistently ignored spontaneous interests or observations from the children, one presumes because they are not part of her programmed day. It seems that her schedule just does not allow room for developing unplanned interests or unanticipated events. When in reply to her question about the kind of bird which made the nest the boy said, "My friend says it's a rain bird" Edith does not inquire further, probably because this does not fit any of her adult categories of birds. The children then express great interest in an object in the nest, but Edith again ignores it—probably it is of no interest to her. The toy soldiers from "Babes in Toyland" strike a responsive note in the children, but Edith doesn't use this interest for any further discussions. The soldiers are treated in the same way as objects which bring little interest from the children. Finally, at the end of sharing time the child world of interest and perception literally erupts in the class with the recollection of the "spooky house" from the zoo. This has apparently made more of an impression on the children than any of the animals. Edith, however, cannot make any sense out of it herself, and her tightly imposed order begins to break down as the children discover a universe of discourse of their own and begin talking excitedly to one another. Edith is completely excluded from this child's world of perception and for a moment she fails to dominate the classroom situation. There are no "spooky houses" planned into Edith's day, and she regains control of the class by beginning the next activity.

Edith gets up from her chair and goes to the book corner, where she puts a record on the phonograph. It is 1:10 as the record begins a story about a trip to the zoo, and she returns to the circle and asks the children to go sit at their tables. They all go and sit on chairs around the four round tables, five or six to a table. When they are all seated Edith asks, "Who wants to be the first one?" One of the girls who has been talking most loudly comes to the center of the room. A voice on the record is giving directions for imitating an ostrich, and the girl follows them, walking around the center of the room bent over holding her ankles. Edith replays the record, and all the children, table by table, imitate ostriches down the center of the room and back. Edith removes her shoes and shows that she can be an ostrich too. This is apparently a familiar game, for a number of children are calling out, "Can we have the crab?" Edith asks one to do a crab "so we can all remember how," and then plays the part of the record with music for imitating crabs by. Table by table, the children slither down the room and back upside-down. The children love this; they run from their tables, dance about waiting for their turns, and are generally exuberant. After the crab they clamor for the "inchworm," and the game is played again, with all the class in turn squirming down the floor. As a conclusion Edith shows them a new animal imitation, the "lame dog." The children all hobble down the floor and back, to the accompaniment of the record.

It is important to see here that Edith has gained control over the class not by building on the children's own newly discovered common interest, but by drawing them into an old game which she knows they like. It seems not to have occurred to Edith to find a meaningful learning experience from this spontaneous interest of the children, perhaps by having them recreate the "spooky house" in the classroom. This would have offered the children a chance for self-expression and creativity, bringing their world of experience into the classroom. Instead, Edith offers them a canned animal imitation procedure which is what she has apparently planned for this part of the day.

At 1:30 Edith takes off the record and comes to the center of the room. She says, "Table one, line up in front of me." The children ask, "What are we going to do?" as they come to the center of the room. She moves two steps to the side and says, "Table two over here, line up next to table one," and more children ask, "What for?" She does this for tables three and four, and each time the children ask, "Why" and "What are we going to do?" When the children are all lined up in four lines spaced so they are not touching one another, Edith puts on a new record and leads the class in the calisthenics which it describes. The children just jump around in their places instead of doing the exercises described, but Edith is so busy doing them she doesn't notice that the children aren't. By the time the record is finished, Edith is exhausted. She is apparently adopting the president's new "physical fitness" program in her classroom.

Here we can see how the children have by this time learned to go smoothly through the teacher-programmed day, whether or not its parts make any sense to them. When they are called to a new procedure such as lining up in the center of the room they ask "Why?" and "What for?" even as they comply with the teacher's directive. They seem to have learned that being in school really does involve "doing what you're told and never mind why." Activities which might make sense to the children because they spring from their spontaneous interest are effectively ruled out in such a rigidly structured situation, and the children are put through senseless activities (from their point of view) by the sheer authority of the teacher. Work time, which comes next in Edith's day, shows how the children act when allowed a chance to choose from among the activities available in the room.

At 1:35 Edith pulls her chair to the easels and calls the children to come and sit on the floor in front of her, table by table. When all are seated she asks, "What are you going to do for work time today?" It seems work time is for drawing, for different children raise their hands and tell Edith what they are going to draw. Most are going to draw animals they saw at the zoo. Edith asks if they want to make pictures to send to Mark in the hospital. Some seem to agree to this. Edith gives the drawing paper to the children, calling them to her one by one. After this the children go to the crayon box to select colors for their pictures, then go to their tables and begin drawing. Edith is again trying to quiet the perpetually talking girls. She keeps two of them standing by her so they won't disrupt the others. She asks them, "Why do you feel you have to talk all the time?" and scolds them for not listening to her. Then she sends them to their tables to draw.

Most of the children are drawing at their tables, sitting or kneeling on their chairs. They are all working very industriously and, engrossed in their work, very quietly. Three girls have chosen to paint at the easels, and having put on smocks, they are mixing bright colors and applying them intently to their pictures. If the children at the tables are the class primitives and neorealists with their animal depictions, these girls at the easels are the abstract-expressionists, with their colorful, broad-stroked paintings.

Edith asks what color she should make the covers for Mark's book, and some children suggest brown and green "because Mark likes them" while others ask, "What book?" and "What does she mean?" Edith again explains they are going to put their drawings in a book to send Mark in the hospital. She sits at a small table in the play kitchen and tells the class to bring her their pictures when they are finished and she will write their messages for Mark on them.

By 1:50 most children have finished their pictures and given them to Edith. She talks with some of them as she ties the bundle together. Children are playing in various parts of the room with toys, games, and blocks which they have taken off the shelves. Some go from table to table examining each other's pictures, offering compliments and suggestions. Three girls at a table are cutting up colored paper for a large collage. Another girl is walking about the room in a pair of high heels with a woman's purse over her arm. Three boys are playing in the center of the room with the large block set, building walkways and walking on them. Edith is very much concerned about their safety and comes over a number of times to fuss over them. Two or three other boys are driving toy trucks around the center of the room, and mild altercations occur when they drive through the block constructions. Some boys and girls are playing at the toy store, two girls are "serving tea" in the play kitchen, and one is washing a baby doll. Two boys have elected to clean the room, and with large sponges they wash the movable blackboard, the puppet stage, and then begin on the tables. They run into resistance from the children who are working with construction toys on the tables and do not want to dismantle their structures. The class is like a room full of bees, each intent on pursuing some activity, occasionally bumping into one another, but then veering off in another direction without serious conflict. The custodian arrives pushing a cart loaded with half-pint milk containers. He places a tray of cartons on the counter next to the sink and leaves. His coming and going is unnoticed in the room, as is the presence of the observer, who is completely ignored by the children for the entire afternoon.

At 2:15 Edith walks to the entrance of the room, switches off the lights, and sits at the piano and plays. The children immediately begin singing the song, which is, "Clean up, clean up, everybody clean up." They begin putting their toys and games back on the shelves under the window. Edith walks around the room urging the rest to shelve their work. "It's clean-up time," she says. When they have put their things away the children go and sit at their tables and wait expectantly. Edith then calls them, table by table, to come wash their hands and get their milk. When all the children are seated at tables with milk, Edith puts on a record and shows the children pictures from a book which goes with it. It is called "Bozo and the Birds" and is the account of the different kinds of birds the clown Bozo meets on a walk through the woods. As the children finish their milk they take pads or blankets from the shelves and lie on them in the center of the room, where Edith sits on her chair showing the pictures. The record ends at 2:40, and Edith says, "Children, down on your blankets." All the class is lying on the floor now. She refuses to answer questions from the children because, she tells them, "It's rest time now." Instead she talks about what they are going to do tomorrow. They are going to work with clay, she says. The children lie quietly and listen. Finally one child raises his hand and tells Edith, "The animals in the zoo looked so hungry yesterday." Edith asks the children about this and a number try to volunteer opinions, but she accepts only those offered in what she calls a "rest time tone," that is, softly and quietly. After a brief discussion of animal feeding, Edith calls the names of two children on milk detail and has them collect the empty cartons from the tables. She asks two children on clean-up detail to straighten up the room. Then she goes and turns on the lights. At this signal the children all get up from the floor, return their blankets to the shelves, and sit at their tables. It is 2:50 when Edith sits at the piano and plays. The children sing a repertoire of songs about animals, including one in which each child sings a refrain alone. They sing right through the 2:55 bell. When the song is finished Edith gets up and says, "Okay, rhyming words to get your coats to-day." The children raise their hands and tell Edith two rhyming words when she calls on them, they go get their coats and sweaters from the hooks in the hall. They return with these and sit at their tables. At 2:59 Edith says, "When you have your coats on, you may line up at the door." Half the children go to the door and stand in a long line. When the 3:00 bell rings Edith returns to the piano and plays. The class sings a song called "Goodbye," after which Edith sends them out.

The social structure Edith has created in this room is a formidable molder of children's behavior and attitudes. She has established a complete set of routines and rituals for controlling the behavior of most of the children for most of the time they are in the room. The children, by the end of the year, have learned the elaborate rules and procedures, so that they move through the day automatically, in response to Edith's signals, from one routine to another, such as from work time to cleanup time. The children are occasionally allowed to choose within this framework, as between one song and another or between drawing and painting. There is, however, no room in this classroom organization for introducing any material from the spontaneous interests of the children. They are organized into a completely teacher-dominated group in which there is no provision for them to make significant contributions to the day's activities.

In such a rigidly structured situation, children's perceptions of the world and opportunities for spontaneous, creative activity are systematically reduced in the classroom. At the same time, unquestioned obedience to adult authority and the rote learning of intrinsically meaningless material are being encouraged. Such a classroom trains children to obediently follow meaningless routines imposed by authoritative figures. This, I contend, is the core of the pupil role as taught in this classroom. Here children are being taught the behaviors and attitudes appropriate to education as a form of industrial processing. They learn to conform to the routines through which they are controlled so they can be taught.

Enforcement of the Pupil Role in the Grades
The first learning of the pupil role takes place in the kindergarten. Teachers in the other grades count on the children's having received this "basic training" there, for they will be

asked to submit to authoritatively imposed routines in all the grades. School days in the elementary grades, as we have seen in previous chapters, are very much like those in kindergarten, with academic material substituted for the kindergarten activities as the content of classroom routines. The grade teachers learn, however, that they cannot rely on the children's enacting the pupil role unless they create the appropriate social structure in their classrooms each year. Classroom teachers who stay in the school learn they must create the kind of social structure in which children can enact the pupil role if they are to be able to control them and to teach them the curriculum. Each elementary-school class run by an experienced teacher will, therefore, have a bureaucratic form of organization, for this is the kind of social structure in which children can enact the pupil role. This is why the experienced teachers say they have learned to spend the first part of each year organizing their classes so they can spend the rest of the year teaching.

We have already seen a number of examples of classrooms organized in this way. In the rooms of the experienced production teachers, such as Irene Goodenough in third grade and Joan Dexter in sixth, the children are put through a series of activities planned by the teacher in advance, and even, in Irene's room, listed on the blackboard. The class moves automatically, or on the teacher's signal, from one subject to the next during the school day, just as Edith's kindergarteners moved from one "time" to another. Programmed days in a bureaucratic organization constitute the school experience for children in these rooms.

The craftsman teachers must also create this form of organization in their classrooms, even though their ideology of education is fundamentally antibureaucratic, if their classroom is to show the requisite order and discipline. This fact is, indeed, a principal source of these teachers' discontent with their work. The regimentation of the bureaucratically organized classroom effectively restricts the children's expression of spontaneous interests, on which they would build their teaching program. The rigidity and narrowness of the pupil role as that of a bureaucratic functionary eliminates most of the opportunity for creative self-expression which these teachers regard as part of true learning. Hence the classroom which is effectively organized to control the children in this way is one in which craftsman teachers cannot carry out their kind of education.

Finally, we have seen examples of classrooms in which inexperienced teachers have failed to create a bureaucratic organization and for this reason have serious problems in controlling the children. Alice Davis in the first grade and Dorothy Jones in the fifth both had such disorganized classrooms. In the first grade this disorganization resulted in disorder and confusion among the children and to the injury to one of them. In the fifth grade, lack of teacher-created order led to classroom disorder, open defiance of the teacher, and borderline chaos in the room. Both these women had failed to organize their classrooms bureaucratically before attempting to teach the year's curriculum. As a result the children could not be effectively controlled because they had no structure within which to play their pupil roles. Dorothy has a production orientation, and sees her job as simply imparting the prescribed fifth-grade curriculum to the children. If she learns the techniques of classroom organization she will be able to remain in teaching. Otherwise the disorder of her room will force her to leave or the principal will ask her to resign. Alice, on the other hand, has a craftsman orientation toward teaching. If she learns to organize her class bureaucratically, she will confirm what she already senses—that she won't be able to carry on her kind of education.

Children's Response to the Pupil Role

Observations of children at the Wilbur Wright Elementary School suggest three possible "ideal type" responses to the role of pupil as bureaucrat. These are identification, submission, and rebellion. Children who identify with the pupil role internalize its expectations, and being a good pupil becomes part of their developing self. Children who submit to the requirements of the pupil role but do not identify with it do what work is required to avoid negative sanctions and actively identify in other forms of activity such as their play groups outside of school. Children who rebel against the pupil role refuse to submit to its requirements, rejecting attempts by the school staff to get them to learn and, often, to conform to classroom behavior norms. No systematic measurement of the distribution of these responses was made in the Wright School classrooms, but extensive observations suggest that somewhat less than half the children actively identify with the pupil role and desire to excel in it, that most submit to the role and accept its requirements in varying degrees, and that a few children rebel and refuse to accept the pupil role.

Children who identify with the pupil role are those we have seen actively and enthusiastically participating in classroom activities. These children not only conform to the classroom norms, but attempt to excel in their terms, and as a consequence they become "good pupils." Being a good pupil becomes an important component of their developing self-images. There are almost always more girls than boys in this category, indicating that this role is easier for girls than for boys. These children in the early grades actively participate in the class as learners and as teacher's helpers. In the upper grades they are the ones who learn to administer their own education, becoming, in the school parlance, "independent learners" who "go ahead on their own," teaching themselves part of the required curriculum through the new routines of independent research. What they learn is to be good bureaucrats, and in this way they *are* being prepared for further educational processing and for life in a society whose social activities are carried on mostly in bureaucratic organizations. The observer often has a feeling of falseness, as we have seen, with these children, as if he were watching a caricature of a role performance. Identifying with the pupil role probably involves a degree of alienation from other aspects of the developing self, since the child is internalizing authoritatively imposed attitudes and behaviors and relinquishing the possibility of acting on his own volition in this part of the social world. Playing a bureaucratic role is always a formal, impersonal activity, and to the extent that children identify with this initial bureaucratic role, we should expect them to begin to show characteristic alienation from the self.

Alienation from the self in the pupil role becomes evident to some of the school staff beginning in the fourth grade. It is at this point in development, the curriculum coordinator observed, that "the light goes out of their eyes" and "they cease to be curious, to explore." The fourth grade is where the teachers say they "wean" the children from the close working relationship with them which characterizes the lower grades and try to train them in independent learning, which is actually self-administration of the curriculum. In our terms, the alienated nature of the pupil role is becoming evident in the behavior of children at this time, to such an extent that the educators themselves come to notice it. Wendy Thomas observed that there was a "gap" developing during the elementary school years between what the children were capable of doing and what they actually did in school. As children progress through the elementary school, she observed, they tend to become stereotyped in their responses, producing what they think the teachers expect of them, and originality and spontaneity vanish. As they identify with the pupil role, the children become less and less individuals in the classroom and more and more segmental role players in a formal organization. This is what is involved in the *successful* acquisition of the pupil role.

The majority of children in any classroom seem to comply with the teacher's requirements without the enthusiasm of those who identify with the pupil role. They can be said to be submitting themselves without significant protest to the authoritatively imposed organization of the bureaucratic classroom, performing the pupil role adequately, and finding their most important and interesting activities outside the school. These children will be the "average pupils" in that they will be "on grade level" in achievement. They will comply with the requirements, but have no drive to put in an excellent performance.

These children do not become either the good pupils or the teacher's helpers in the classroom. They do what they are asked, and what is required of them in their grade, but they do not volunteer their active, willing involvement. They reserve their voluntary participation and spontaneous interest for activities outside the classroom, at home or in their play groups. In the lower grades, where they are still treated as children, they may find many satisfying activities in the classroom itself. These would be games and toys and activities they themselves invent when not working directly with the teacher. This opportunity is vastly decreased, however, in the upper grades, where the teachers attempt to make the children self-teaching learners and discourage "childish" forms of behavior. This is probably another source of the disaffection from schoolwork noticed in the upper grades. The unidentified but submissive pupils can no longer find intrinsically interesting activities in the classroom, and the school day becomes a long, tedious ordeal.

The children who submit to the pupil role but do not identify with it provide, especially in the upper grades, a potential source of support for the rebellious pupils when they challenge the authority of the teacher. These are the children who follow the rebels who openly defy Dorothy Jones's authority in her fifth grade, whereas the children who identify with the pupil role remain at their desks holding their ears and trying to get through the assigned work. Children who are rebelling against the pupil role, then, can look to this majority group of submissive students for support if they seem to successfully challenge the teacher's authority and begin to create a counter-organization to hers in the classroom. Most Wilbur Wright teachers knew of instances in which children had successfully defied the teacher, set up their own classroom organization, and prevented the teacher from carrying on instruction. Teachers who found themselves in such situations were forced to go along with the children's organization or resign from their jobs. In the previous two years children had successfully organized classrooms against the teacher and the curriculum in a fifth grade at the nearby Beechwood School and in a second grade at Wright school.

Children who rebel against the pupil role do not learn and often do not conform to the behavioral norms of the classroom organization. Those who refuse to learn the curriculum as is expected of them but do submit to behavioral discipline of the classroom are in passive rebellion. They can score low on the psychologist's aptitude tests, be declared "slow learners," and be taught at a lower level than the rest of the class. In this way they will not be expected to perform up to grade standard, and the teacher need not feel guilty about being unable to educate them. They are not a "problem" to the teacher because they do not misbehave in class and create disturbances.

A clear example of this passive rebellion is seen in a "slow learner" in Joan Dexter's sixth grade. An observer reported his behavior as follows:

The most dramatic example of covert resistance to the pupil role is Tony, one of the stars of the recess baseball game in Joan's class. He is the smallest boy in the class, and makes up for his size with the tremendous amount of energy and enthusiasm he throws into the recess baseball game each day. He is completely involved: he knows everything that is happening on the field, he keeps track of the innings, the outs and strikes on the batter from one day to another so the game can be resumed each day where it left off the previous day. No violation of baseball rules or ethics escapes his notice on the diamond, and his voice is heard calling strategic advice to his teammates, or razzing members of the other team, in a truly professional way. But when Tony walks into the classroom from recess, a most amazing transformation comes over him. His movements become sluggish, he shuffles his feet as he walks, his arms hang slack at his sides, his eyelids drop halfway down over his eyes, and his mouth falls halfway open, so that he looks like the classic picture of the dull child. When asked about him, Joan said kindly that he was "a little below average in ability" and she didn't expect too much of him academically.

This boy has successfully put over the picture of himself as a dull child, so that few academic demands are made on him, when in fact he is probably one of the sharpest children in the class. In our terms, he is in passive rebellion against the pupil role, and has found his personally involving activity in sports. In the classroom he sits and behaves himself and is expected to do little work, but on the baseball diamond he comes to life in a world which is meaningful to him. This child and other passive rebels have chosen to play dumb in order to avoid the demands of the learning aspects of the pupil role.

Whether a child who is in rebellion is passive or aggressive is probably partly due to how he is handled by the teacher. Without the recess baseball game into which to throw all his energies and commit his obviously astute intelligence, Tony might well be making trouble in the classroom, leading the students in rebellion against the teacher-imposed order there rather than leading the boys in baseball for half an hour a day. In the lower grades experienced teachers try to establish a close personal relationship with such children and control their behavior by carefully supervising them during the day. In an upper-grade classroom like Joan's it is possible to control them through a combination of a very rigidly enforced classroom organization and a structured "safety valve" through which their energies and abilities can escape in ways harmless to the teacher's control of the class. The boy in Joan's room, in fact, has been made a functional part of her classroom structure: she never has to bother about supervising the boys at recess. She can always rely on his keeping things going smoothly on the diamond.

Children who are in active rebellion refuse to learn the required curriculum or to conform to the behavioral rules established by the teacher. They are often known as "troublemakers." They are not content to sit through the school day as passive rebels, but are driven to actively challenge the teacher's authority and control. They need to aggressively assert themselves against the organization of the classroom and of the school itself. They must personally violate the rules governing behavior; hence they are usually in trouble with both the teacher and the principal, as well as their parents and authorities in the community.

These active rebels are not content, however, with making a personal nuisance of themselves in school. They often lead others, by example or instigating, in group defiance of classroom rules. They are thus a potential subversive influence in the classroom, always ready to lead at least some of the submissive children in activities which violate the teacher's rules and challenge her authority and control. We have already seen how a girl in Dorothy Jones's fifth grade leads a group of children in defiance of the teacher's rules. This girl is always ready for this kind of defiance, and takes each opportunity to organize some of the class into a group whose norms violate those of the teacher's group organization. Dorothy never breaks this child's defiance, but reasserts her control by creating a confrontation in which the other children desert the rebel and move back toward submission to the teacher's organization. When kept after school for punishment, this child acts in the same way, openly defying Dorothy and trying to get the other children to join her.

The most aggressive of the active rebels in Wright School during the study is a boy in Ruth Tucker's fourth grade. This boy, named Bob, cannot read, write, or do arithmetic. He works from first-grade materials when Ruth can convince him to work, which is very seldom. He spends his days, rather, in a series of systematic violations of the rules of the classroom and the school. Every part of the school day for him is an opportunity to find ways of violating rules and agreements of school social life. At recess, for example, he systematically cheats at all class games. His cheating, however, is subtle; a violation of basic rules which hinders the progress of the game rather than a violent assault on another child. For example, in stoop tag, in which the person tagged is supposed to place his hand on his head and help to tag others, this boy stoops and holds his hand just an inch or two off the top of his head. One never knows whether he is tagged or not. His classroom violations are also subtle and systematically disruptive. When the class is instructed to take out their readers, he turns his first-grade book upside down, holding it up so the teacher cannot miss his defiance. The class has a sign which a child takes when he goes to the toilet, and no one else may go until it is returned to its place. This boy can be counted upon to pocket the sign sometime during the school day.

Bob engages in more openly disruptive behavior which has a disorganizing effect on the class, for it seems to encourage a

few other children to somewhat lesser acts of defiance. He wanders about the room talking when the class is supposed to be working, and creates little groups of talking boys. Ruth breaks up these groups by calling the names of the other boys involved and getting them to return to their seats. The rebel, when called upon to take his seat, defies Ruth by totally ignoring the command or making some outlandish response, such as lying down on the floor. That the boy is not stupid is clearly shown by the cleverness implied in the extremely varied repertoire of defiant acts he has built up over the years. He is, at this point in his school career, an artist in the techniques of flouting authority and defying its social organizations. With his example of total rejection of the pupil role, other rebellious, or just submissive, children are able to move away from the teacher-created organization toward more independent and defiant modes of behavior. They never reach the point of total rejection and defiance that Bob has, but he acts as a social magnet attracting children away from the teacher's organization and toward the establishment of more satisfying forms of social interaction. Not surprisingly, this child is often seen sitting in the school office, having been expelled from class, and by midyear he has been expelled from school.

Children in rebellion against the pupil role, either passively or actively, are usually referred to the school psychologist for testing and whatever help or referral for help he can give them. They generally test low in intelligence and ability, but this should be seen as part of their role rejection. They don't do well in class and they don't do well on out-of-class aptitude tests; they are rejecting the entire school organization and all its parts. The psychologist is a resource for these teachers in trying to deal with rebels. When the psychologist can tell a teacher like Joan Dexter that the student who is not learning in her room has a low aptitude, she can, as we have seen, feel justified in not asking him to learn much during the year. A child like the boy in Ruth Tucker's room, however, is more difficult, for the teacher must also ask the psychologist to help her find ways of controlling him in the classroom. The Wright School psychologist, who also works at three other elementary

schools, gives what time he can to therapy with such a boy, but he knows this is not enough, and therefore tries to get the parents to have the child treated privately. This is all he can do under the present conditions of his work.

7

Conclusions

The theme of this study has been the interplay of ideology, social structure, and social action in the elementary school program. We have reached the conclusion that only a limited range of ideas and practices are congruent with the underlying bureaucratic structure of the school and can be realized, whereas those outside this range are at variance with the organizational structure and cannot be realized, and people who hold to them have to find ways of adjusting to this failure. Specifically, it has been found that an industrial ideology of education and a production type of classroom teaching can be implemented in the elementary school, whereas an individualistic ideology and craftsman practice of education cannot. The school staff members who hold the individualistic philosophy and attempt to practice craftsman teaching must find ways of adjusting to frustration and failure in their work.

At least three forms of adjustment to the failure to realize individualistic goals in a bureaucratic setting are illustrated in the Brookview school system: These are leaving the organization, redefining one's goals, and becoming so involved in pressing administrative work as to be distracted from activities related to individualistic goals. Those who leave the organization do so with feelings of personal failure and of frustration with the organization itself. Those who redefine their goals must either convince themselves that the other ideologies are more worthwhile than the ones they hold or, perhaps more likely, allow themselves to become convinced over time that the actions they *can* take in the organization actually constitute realization of their original goals. Those who become involved in distracting administrative tasks can console themselves for a time that, although they are not working directly toward their individualistic goals, they are working to create the conditions in which this will eventually be possible.

To recapitulate, the administrators of education in Brookview, Wright School, and Seaboard State subscribe to a liberal, humanitarian and individualistic philosophy of education. These men, including Superintendent of Schools Robert Nelson, Curriculum Coordinator Saul Levine, Wright School Principal Hyram Johnson, and the commissioner in the Seaboard State Department of Education, see the public schools as ideally one of the important social means for implementing the democratic, individualistic, progressive values of Western civilization. The schools give everyone a chance for education, so that those with ability and motivation, regardless of their social background, have access to responsible, high-status positions in society. This, these educators feel, is to the benefit of society and of the individual. Public schools, in this philosophy, are created for service to individuals; school personnel are dedicated to helping children realize their individual potential for development, and do not try to force a uniform, standardized development on all children. By facilitating self-realization, schools can contribute to the development of healthy, happy, productive people with integrated value systems and strong autonomous personalities. Such people, these educators believe, cannot help but create a better world when they grow up and take their places in society.

The organization through which they seek to implement this philosophy of education is, of course, the bureaucracy of the Brookview school system and the bureaucratic structures of the individual schools. These organizations have standardized procedures, programs, and goals to which all participants are expected to conform. The most important of these in its consequences for the goals of the educators is the prescribed year-by-year school-system curriculum. The subject matter which the children are expected to learn at each grade level, and the procedures recommended for teaching it, are specified in the school-system *Curriculum Guides*. A general testing program for all the schools in the system provides a quality control mechanism for assessing how well children have learned the required curriculum. The basic task of the professional people in the schools is to facilitate children's mastery of the standardized school system curriculum.

An industrial analogy has been suggested as appropriate to the kind of educational process implied in the standardized curriculum and its enforcement through the testing program. In this analogy, the school system can be conceived of as a series of stages of production in which children, as the raw materials, are subjected to uniform processing in order to produce a set of standardized educational products. To the extent that the Brookview school system resembles this industrial model of education, the realization of the goals of the educational administrators becomes impossible.

The study has shown that the forces at work within the school bureaucracy and outside of it in the community tend to move education toward this industrial model. This means that the educational administrators must find ways of adjusting their individualistic goals to the bureaucratic realities of their work situation. They do this in a number of ways. The state com-

missioner engages in a propaganda campaign against this form
of education and administers his department so as to encourage
creativity and innovation on the level of the local school systems. However, his most effective adjustment probably comes
through his complete involvement in the details of administering the state department of education. Superintendent of Schools
Robert Nelson also delegates as much decision-making authority as he can to his principals, and works at gaining community acceptance for his ideology of education. However, he
too can become completely absorbed in the details of running
the school system, including involvement in community educational politics, to the extent that he can define the passing of
the annual school budget, the approval of a bond issue for an
addition to the high school, or the election of a friendly liberal
to the chairmanship of the board of education as a major vic-
tory for education, since they enable him to keep the system
operating. Keeping the system operating can, of course, be seen
as a necessary prerequisite to the realization of any individualistic education goals. Saul Levine, the curriculum supervisor, applies himself to "educating" the public to this liberal humanitarian and individualistic philosophy of education; to training
the faculty members in its implementation; and to organizing
faculty committees to revise the *Curriculum Guides* so they will
be more in line with this philosophy. Of all the administrators,
his day-to-day work is probably most closely connected with
the attempt to realize his goals for education, and he seems
to experience more continued frustration than any of the others.

Principal Johnson at Wright School also uses or considers
using all these means of adjusting to the frustrations of his
work. He is trying to implement an individualistic philosophy of
education in a particular school, which of course is a bureacracy
within a larger bureaucracy, and so he has two sources of pressure toward standardization. Johnson concentrates on profes-
sionalizing the working conditions of the school and the attitudes of the staff, which can be considered as a prerequisite to
developing any kind of high-quality educational program. He
tries to rationalize education at Wright School—that is, to find
the most efficient and effective ways of teaching the required

school system curriculum. This effort might be seen as a direct contribution to the further industrialization of education, but Johnson defines it instead as keeping the school up to date and thereby providing the children with the best available education. Finally, Johnson attempts to individualize instruction in the required subject matter by having the teachers administer the standard curriculum on the basis of the child's capacity for mastering it rather than the formal grade-level prescriptions. In doing so, he says he is encouraging individualized instruction, and opens the possibility of eventually coming to equate this with his ideal of individual education. The two are, of course, quite different; but if Johnson eventually comes to equate them in his own mind he will have successfully redefined his professional goals. There is also the possibility of leaving the organization. He can, as he pointed out one day, get a doctorate as an "insurance policy" so he can get a job teaching college if he ever leaves educational administration.

When the bureaucratic organization and the industrial type of program are combined with effectively organized pressures from the community for economy and businesslike efficiency in the school system, the situation may very well become intolerable for educators like Nelson, Levine, and Johnson. During the study of the Brookview schools, the conservative educational party was successful in defeating the school budget in the popular vote and, in the following election, in capturing a majority of seats on the board of education. The cut in expenditures necessitated by the defeat of the administration's budget ended programs especially favored by Nelson and Levine. They interpreted this as a popular rejection of their policies and goals. The election of conservatives who openly opposed them and their ideas to a majority on the board confirmed them in their feeling of popular rejection. At the end of the study, Nelson left Brookview to become superintendent of the school system in a nearby town experiencing the kind of rapid population growth Brookview was undergoing when he came to work there. This meant, in effect, that he could count on spending at least the next five years completely involved in the problems of providing minimum adequate physical facili-

ties for education in this town. He was going there to "build up
that school system," as he said, and he meant it literally in
terms of involvement in financing, designing, locating, and con-
structing new school buildings. Levine was actively looking for
a school system in which he could carry on the type of educational work he valued. Johnson was staying at Wright School
and hoping he would be able to continue to realize some of his
educational goals under the new superintendent of schools.

The craftsman teachers at Wilbur Wright Elementary School
are the other group of educators with an individualistic ideology. They feel that the school curriculum should be designed
for the children in each class each year, so that every child is
taught what he "needs to know" when he is "ready to learn it."
They would teach the skills and knowledge of the elementary
school years as parts of educational programs developed out of
the interests of the children in their rooms. Ideally, for these
teachers, schoolwork would be an integral part of the children's
experience, since it developed out of their spontaneous interests,
and learning would be an act of creative self-expression, mastering part of the child's real world. They want to establish the
kind of personal relationship with each child which will enable
them to know the child's abilities and interests and to create
experiences which will stimulate curiosity and genuine learning.
The craftsman orientation toward teaching would be a way to
realize the individualistic philosophy in the classroom.

Teachers with this individualistic orientation toward teaching immediately found themselves in conflict with the requirements of the standard school-system curriculum, which they
were responsible for imparting to their children, at least to the
extent of the acceptable minimum achievement levels in the
system. Before he would approve their innovative classroom
programs, Principal Johnson required assurances from the
teachers that the children would learn the formal curriculum
during the year. Parents, too, were very fearful of their procedures, because they felt that their children would not learn
as much in their classrooms. The children themselves were not
accustomed to education organized on the basis of their own

interests and had to be taught how to make classroom activities part of their everyday lives. The craftsman teachers were thus under considerable pressure from many different sources to teach the standard curriculum.

Resisting the pressure toward standardization in the classroom and creating individual education required a great deal of energy and courage from the craftsman teachers. But what ultimately made their work impossible was probably the organization all teachers had to create in the classroom to control the children so they could teach them. All teachers, whether they had a production orientation or a craftsman orientation, discovered after a year of work that they had to organize their classrooms as little bureaucracies if they were to control the children sufficiently to teach them the required curriculum and enforce the required order, cleanliness, and quiet. In the course of the study we discovered that experienced teachers of both orientations created formal organizations to fulfill these requirements of the school system. These effectively negated the fundamental premise of the craftsman teacher—that she could establish a personal relationship with each child through which she could discover his learning needs and the ways in which he could best be taught.

The problem of classroom organization, added to the pressures from principal, parents, and children and the inexorable demands of the curriculum, make the work of craftsman teachers impossible. Three of the four at Wright School were leaving classroom teaching at the end of the study. Becky Yager, the most experienced and knowledgeable of these teachers, was taking the position of general advisory teacher at Wright School. Robert Paul was studying at nights to become a school psychologist, and would leave the classroom as soon as he had sufficient credits. Hannah Gilbert left teaching at the end of the year and did not know if she would ever return in any capacity. Only Alice Davis, the most inexperienced of the craftsman teachers, planned to remain in the classroom at the end of the study. The radically individualized education which these teachers believe in and attempt to put into practice in the class-

room seems impossible to any significant extent in the structure of the Brookview school system or, by implication, in any
large-scale bureaucratic educational organization.

Teachers with a production orientation, on the other hand,
can adjust readily to the classroom situation and be successful
in the terms of the educational organization. Their goal is imparting the required curriculum to the children in their classes,
and is thus consistent with the bureaucratic requirements of
the educational system. They receive help from the special
teachers and the principal in working out efficient, effective
programs for teaching children the required subject matter.
The work of the production teachers can be said to significantly
reinforce the tendencies toward the industrialization of the educational process in Brookview.

The attitudes of the parents toward education generally reinforce the other tendencies toward the industrial model of
education in the Brookview school system. The vast majority
desire the most efficient education the schools can give their
children in terms of teaching what they consider basic academic subjects. They tend to think of the learning process in
very traditional terms as children sitting at their desks working
from books. They have no understanding of the craftsman form
of teaching and are unable to conceive of how children could
learn from a curriculum developed out of their own interests
by a creative and intelligent teacher. They are unsympathetic
even with the forms of individualized instruction and programs
for the rationalization of education developed by Principal
Johnson. To them, small-group work in the classroom means
that the children in the rest of the class are not learning, and
instructional units involve all sorts of activities which do not
seem to them to be "educational." Johnson and the educators
with his goals and philosophy are therefore caught between two
powerful forces: the bureaucratic structure of the school system
which demands standardization of learning and the demands of
the parents for the traditional *forms* of learning as well as the
industrylike goals of efficiency and standardization.

For the children, participating in school means essentially becoming bureaucratic role-players in the classroom. We have found that the children respond in at least three different ways to the definition of the pupil role as that of bureaucratic functionary. Some identify with this role, incorporate its component behaviors and attitudes into their developing self-images, and become good pupils. A majority of children seem to submit to the demands of the role, conform outwardly to its requirements, learn what is expected of them, and become the average pupils. A few children rebel against the demands of the pupil role and refuse to conform to its requirements. They do not learn what is expected of them, and become slow pupils. Some refuse to conform to classroom discipline and become the school's problem children. The bureaucratic role of pupil helps prepare the good pupils for life in a society of large-scale organizations, but it provides the children in general with little opportunity to develop as individuals, which is the goal of the educators who subscribe to the individualistic philosophy of education and the teachers with the craftsman orientation. The structural forces at work in the school system overwhelm the attempts of these educators to implement their ideologies. The bureaucratic social organization of the school seems to rule out implementation of their individualistic philosophy and practice of education.

Bibliography

The following bibliography includes books and articles on elementary education, the sociology of education, the sociology of organizations, and the few materials that are available on the social organization of schools and classrooms. The latter are extremely scarce, consisting of a mere handful of theoretical and empirical works which attempt to relate the organization of schools and classrooms to the teaching and learning which occurs within them. For a long time, the standard work on the sociology of education has been Brookover and Gottlieb, *A Sociology of Education*, first published in the 1950s and now in a second edition; it has now been joined by an equally good overview of the field by Banks, *The Sociology of Education*, published in 1968.

The classic statement of the sociology of education is probably Durkheim's *Education and Sociology*, and Brim's *Sociology and the Field of Education* has served to show contemporary relationships between the fields. Willard Waller's *The Sociology of Teaching* is a classic in its field and perhaps the best modern study of education.

There is, of course, a plethora of books on elementary education per se, and I have listed only those which I found particularly helpful in orienting a sociologist to this field. Background reading on modern education necessarily includes the works by John Dewey, Lawrence Cremin, and Lucy Sprague Mitchell. Dahlke's *Values in Culture and Classroom* and Mayer's *The Schools* deal in quite different ways with the relationship of classroom structure to learning and teaching, and both are valuable in a field where there is so little available, as are Henry's observations from the classroom in his articles and in his *Culture against Man*. The articles listed by Bidwell, Parsons, Getzels and Thelen, and Lippitt and Gold provide useful perspectives on the school and classroom as social systems. Recent highly critical popular works, such as those by Kohl, Silberman, and Le Shan also touch on the relation of structure to teaching and learning.

I have found a few studies of other formal organizations to be useful examples of the kind of analysis undertaken here, which relates organization structure to the performance of its task. These include most importantly Stanton and Schwartz, *The Mental Hospital*, Blau and Scott, *Formal Organizations*, and Gouldner, *Patterns of Industrial Bureaucracy*.

Books

Anderson, James G. *Bureaucracy in Education*. Baltimore: Johns Hopkins University Press, 1968.

Banks, Olive. *The Sociology of Education*. New York: Schocken Books, 1968.

Blau, Peter M., and Scott, W. R. *Formal Organizations*. San Francisco: Chandler, 1962.

Brim, Orvil G. *Sociology and the Field of Education*. New York: Russell Sage Foundation, 1958.

Brookover, Wilbur A., and Gottlieb, David. *A Sociology of Education*. 2d ed. New York: American Book Company, 1964.

Carmien, Laiten. *Education: The Process and the Social Institution*. New York: Vantage Press, 1964.

Caplow, Theodore. *Principles of Organization.* New York: Harcourt, Brace and World, 1964.

Cicourel, Aaron V., and Kitsuse, John J. *The Educational Decision-makers.* Indianapolis: Bobbs-Merrill, 1963.

Cremin, Lawrence. *Transformation of the Schools.* New York: Alfred A. Knopf, 1961.

Dahlke, H. Otto. *Values in Culture and Classroom.* New York: Harper and Row, 1958.

Dewey, John. *Experience and Education.* New York: Macmillan Co., 1938.

————. *The School and the Child.* London: Blackie and Son, 1907.

Dexter, Lewis. *The Tyranny of Schooling: An Inquiry into the Problem of "Stupidity."* New York: Basic Books, 1964.

Durkheim, Emile. *Education and Sociology.* Translated by Sherwood D. Fox. New York: Free Press, 1956.

Etzioni, Amitai. *Modern Organizations.* Englewood Cliffs, New Jersey: Prentice-Hall, 1964.

Gouldner, Alvin W. *Patterns of Industrial Bureaucracy.* New York: Free Press, 1954.

Havighurst, Robert J., and Neugarten, Bernice L. *Society and Education.* Boston: Allyn and Bacon, 1957.

Henry, Jules. *Culture against Man.* New York: Random House, 1963.

Kohl, Herbert R. *The Open Classroom: A Practical Guide to a New Way of Teaching.* New York: New York Review (Vintage Books), 1970.

————. *Thirty-six Children.* New York: New American Library, 1967.

Le Shan, Eda. *The Conspiracy against Childhood.* New York: Atheneum, 1967.

Mayer, Martin. *The Schools.* New York: Harper and Row, 1961.

Mead, Margaret. *The School in American Culture.* Cambridge: Harvard University Press, 1955.

Merton, Robert K., and others. *Reader in Bureaucracy.* New York: Free Press, 1952.

Mitchell, Lucy Sprague. *Our Children and Our Schools.* New York: Simon and Schuster, 1950.

Rugg, Harold, and Shumaker, Ann. *The Child-centered School: An Appraisal of the New Education.* Yonkers-on-Hudson: World Book Co., 1928.

Seeley, John R.; Sim, R. Alexander; and Loosely, E. W. *Crestwood Heights.* New York: Basic Books, 1956.

Silberman, Charles E. *Crisis in the Classroom.* New York: Random House, 1970.

Stanton, Alfred H., and Schwartz, Morris S. *The Mental Hospital.* New York: Basic Books, 1954.

Waller, Willard. *The Sociology of Teaching.* New York: John Wiley, 1932.

Articles

Bidwell, Charles E. "The School as a Formal Organization." In *Handbook of Organizations,* edited by James G. March, pp. 972–1002. Chicago: Rand McNally, 1965.

Getzels, J. W., and Thelen, H. A. "The Classroom as a Unique Social System." *National Society for the Study of Education Yearbook* 59 (1960): 53–81.

Glazer, Nathan. "Three Possible Contributions of Sociology to Education." *Journal of Educational Sociology* 33 (1959): 97–104.

Gouldner, Alvin W. "Organizational Analysis." In *Sociology Today,* edited by Robert K. Merton and others, pp. 400–428. New York: Basic Books, 1959.

Gross, Neal. "Sociology of Education." In *Sociology Today,* edited by Robert K. Merton and others, pp. 128–52. New York: Basic Books, 1959.

Henry, Jules. "American Classrooms: Learning the Nightmare." *Columbia University Forum,* spring 1963, pp. 24–30.

————. "Docility: On Giving the Teacher What She Wants." *Journal of Social Issues* 11 (1955): 33–54.

Lippitt, Roland, and Gold, M. "Classroom Social Structure as a Mental Health Problem." *Journal of Social Issues* 15 (1959): 40–49.

Parsons, Talcott. "The School Class as a Social System: Some of Its Functions in American Society." *Harvard Educational Review* 29 (1959): 297–318.

Strauss, Anselm. "A Sociological Approach to Educational Organization." *School Review* 65 (1957): 330–38.

Wilson, Burton R. "The Teacher's Role: A Sociological Analysis." *British Journal of Sociology* 13 (1962): 15–32.

Index